ENDOR_____

One of my great honors in life and ministry was to meet C. Peter Wagner and work alongside him on many occasions. He was a man of deep integrity and revelatory wisdom, a true servant of the Lord. He has had an amazing impact on the church all around the world. His gifts were many, and his ability to lead and inspire was legendary. But I'd like to suggest that Peter Wagner's true mark of greatness was his unwavering faithfulness to the end. And now we are given this profound book, which he wrote together with his amazing wife, Doris: *6 Secrets to Living a Fruitful Life*. They could write it because they lived it. This book comes with great wisdom and insight. But even more than that, it comes with an impartation of grace to live the same fruitful life they did. Read it and enjoy it—and let's run together into this increased lifestyle of fruitfulness.

BILL JOHNSON
Bethel Church, Redding, California
Author of *The Way of Life* and *Born for Significance*

Peter Wagner was a pioneer of faith. The impact that his life left on mine was unparalleled, as a spiritual father, mentor, and apostolic leader in the Body of Christ. As part of his legacy, Peter wrote a multitude of books and invaluable teachings that have blessed the global Church in countless ways. True to his nature, this final book in his collection imparts keys of wisdom that he accumulated during his rich lifelong experience. I heartily recommend *6 Secrets to Living a Fruitful Life* because it carries Peter's heart to equip believers for the work of ministry, while adding one more layer to the indelible legacy of a man of God who truly finished well.

Dr. Ché Ahn
Founder and President, Harvest International Ministry
Founding and Senior Pastor, Harvest
Rock Church, Pasadena, California
International Chancellor, Wagner University
Founder, Ché Ahn Ministries

I counted Peter as a close personal friend and his wife, Doris, remains so today. Peter was a gift to the Body of Christ globally. He set a standard of excellence in life and leadership for each of us to emulate. Peter left us a wealth of wisdom in his books, and I am grateful to follow in his footsteps as we continue on the path he pioneered for us. In this, his last book, he gives us the sure and true road map for living life in the abundant fruitfulness of God. The pages are filled with reminders of his humor, wit, and profound wisdom gained by a life well lived. Peter, you are greatly missed. Live on in your writings. Thank you, Doris, for bringing this book to print.

Jane Hansen Hoyt
Aglow International

I've only had a few mentors in my life and the wisest, most generous of them was Dr. C. Peter Wagner. The first thing he told me was "Just call me Peter," but now I can honor him properly as a father, scholar, pioneer, and a teacher's teacher. This book is probably his most valuable, as when you come to the twilight of your years you have a fresh perspective on the most important lessons to pass on. The chapter "Pick Your Battles" could save you from a major trap. And "Pursue Convergence" is the chapter people need more than any other as it describes a phenomena only 20 percent of ministries experience, and the researcher, Dr. J. Robert (Bobby) Clinton, used Peter as his model. I read "Dull a Sharp Tongue" before, but realized I needed to read it again. Every chapter is a mine with gems hidden inside. Hebrews 11 lists the heroes of faith and Dr. C. Peter Wagner walks among them. As it was written of them, it can be said that through this book, Peter, "being dead yet speaketh." You'll want to listen to what he says.

LANCE WALLNAU
CEO, Lance Learning Group
Dallas, Texas

Wow! I loved reviewing this book. It is Peter through and through. Peter was a great man, brilliant, world renowned. He also was a gracious, loving, encouraging, gentle, embracing man. He was a true father, always seeing the best in us. He also was a very practical man and talked to those of us who were close to him about living successfully in practical matters. He talked about wills, successors, as well as cutting-edge thoughts about where the church was going and how we should be thinking. I loved being in his and Doris' presence. This book reflects everything about Peter so well. I was so blessed to be one of those in his closer group and to have known him not only as a leader but as a friend. This book is C. Peter Wagner through and through! It's the man I knew and revere today and every day! This book explains not only how to finish well but how to live successfully daily! Every leader needs this book. This is genuine Peter Wagner!

BARBARA J. YODER
Lead Apostle, Shekinah
Regional Apostolic Center

C. Peter Wagner, a man of God who blessed the Body of Christ more than most Christian ministries. Peter's driving passion was to use his influence and divine giftings to help others succeed in their callings and be and do their best for the Kingdom. Because of his spirit and attitude and special gifted abilities, he developed eight major Christian organizations that became worldwide in their ministries. At 80 years of age, Peter released those ministries to the men and women he had helped train and inspire to build successful works that blessed the Body of Christ.

Though I had worked with restoring apostles and prophets into the church since 1954, when Peter started the International Coalition of Apostles, I gladly joined with Peter to promote the modern-day apostles. Peter was a humble man with faith and vision to accept and advance in restored truth and dare to do the difficult challenges. Peter became a very close friend and wrote Forewords for several of my books. At 86 years of age and 67 years of ministry, I look forward to the day I will be joining with Peter and the great cloud of witnesses to fulfill God's eternal purpose throughout eternity. Bless all whom Peter loved and labored with in God's Kingdom. This book is full of wisdom like the book of Proverbs and the greatest New Testament truths. This book is a classic of Kingdom principles, practical sayings, and many other valuables that will help readers grow in grace and knowledge of the Lord Jesus Christ.

BISHOP BILL HAMON

Christian International Apostolic-Global Network
Author of *The Eternal Church, Prophets & Personal Prophecy, Prophets & the Prophetic Movement, Prophets, Pitfalls, & Principles, Apostles/Prophets & the Coming Moves of God, The Day of the Saints, Who Am I & Why Am I Here, Prophetic Scriptures Yet to be Fulfilled (3rd Reformation), 70 Reasons for Speaking in Tongues, How Can These Things Be?, God's Weapons of War,* and *Your Highest Calling*

C. Peter Wagner was a man who not only changed my life, but he changed the lives of many thousands of people around the world! Peter was known and respected as a powerful teacher. He was loved not merely because of his sincere friendship. He was also loved and is remembered for his love of humor. Who could forget Peter's jokes that he told before each of his teachings? *6 Secrets to Living a Fruitful Life* is Peter's last book. He, along with his wife, Doris, provide the reader a pathway to a life lived and ended with God's blessings. Practical as well as spiritual secrets, or guidelines, are given in this book for success in life. These secrets help each reader to progress through life and finish a life well lived! Peter's legacy will continue through the generations as this book is read and the lessons are applied. Begin today to implement the *6 Secrets to Living a Fruitful Life* and create a lasting legacy for your own family and followers!

BARBARA WENTROBLE
President, International Breakthrough Ministries
President, Breakthrough Business leaders
Author and Speaker

Good leadership leaves a legacy of wisdom, godly counsel, and practical experiences. Peter Wagner, with the help of Doris, has provided that legacy gift in *6 Secrets to Living a Fruitful Life*. It is compiled of important aspects for each of our lives that, if applied, can lead you to a successful and fulfilling life...finishing well. No matter your age or path in life, this book has wisdom for you. I love Peter and Doris so much. I am honored to be connected with the Wagners and to be a recipient of the wisdom and life experiences he shares. He "finished well" and left us keys to how we too can finish well. I encourage you to read and reread this book to help you stay focused and lead a productive and joy-filled life!

DR. JOHN BENEFIEL
Presiding Apostle, Heartland Apostolic Network
Senior Pastor, Church on the Rock

I consider it one of the highest privileges to date in my adult life to be invited to endorse the final manuscript of C. Peter Wagner. My husband, Greg, and I love him and Doris dearly. They are family to us and we count it a joy, privilege, and honor that the Lord made a way for Peter and Doris to be spiritual mentors and parents in our lives. As I read this manuscript, I laughed, cried, and learned all over again. As one who has run closely with Peter for many years, this book so greatly expresses the true character and essence of who he was, how he truly lived his life, and what he modeled well. I can hear Peter's voice as I have, to date, read through the pages of this book three times. All the wonderful principles we learned and gleaned from him laid out so well.

Friend, he genuinely lived what he taught. What you saw is what you got. Peter was the real deal. Genuine, so generous, caring, honest, kind, full of joy, never complained, brilliant, wise, fun, a fearless, yet humble, apostolic father and pioneer. Not only did Peter instruct through his teachings and writings, Peter taught through how he lived life. He writes in the book how he wanted to be remembered: "I (Peter Wagner) want to be remembered as one who, over the years, accurately heard what the Spirit was saying to the churches, and who faithfully communicated it to leaders of the Body of Christ." And oh, how well he did this throughout his lifetime of ministry.

But I also want to state that Peter is also remembered as and will always be a father. He was and is my spiritual father. He was not only a father to a few, but to many. He impacted Christian leaders throughout the nations of the world, yet was a truly approachable and kind man. He and Doris have pioneered movement upon movement that have brought Kingdom-of-God history to the countries worldwide. And had such fun and joy in doing it!

Peter, you indeed set your face toward the goal and with steadfast resolve and faith have run your race; and, in my humble opinion, have finished it beyond exceptionally well. I know you are cheering all of us on from the great cloud of witnesses. It is an honor to carry on the legacy you left all of your spiritual sons and daughters. And it is my prayer that even as we continue to impact nations following behind in your stead, that twenty, thirty years from now, people whose lives we are impacting will have this to say, "We did not know Peter or Doris Wagner personally, but how those carrying on their torch of what was taught, modeled, and imparted is so evident in their lives and ministries that we honor the legacy of this couple."

Thank you, Peter, and most importantly thank you, Lord, for the great honor and joy it has been and is to be a Wagner spiritual kid. You taught me to truly be me, you stretched me out of comfort zones and encouraged me to write. You opened doors to ministry and destiny, you introduced me to many who are now lifelong friends and ministry partners. You encouraged us and so many others multiple times with the following statement, "Darlin', go further and farther than we ever did."

You encouraged the prophetic warrior in me to be bold and wise. We are choosing our battles wisely as you so often reminded us to do. We are awakening a generation to spiritual warfare as you always said, "Each generation must learn to war (spiritual warfare)." You modeled a true apostle, one who could truly father the one in front of him and then from the platform or at that roundtable leadership meeting speak a message that would birth movements and father nations. You are remembered daily and loved and honored, always Peter.

Doris, what an amazing job you have done in the scribing of this manuscript. Thank you. Friend, *6 Secrets to Living a Fruitful Life* is a must-read for all believers and even more strategic, a message for all leaders and true apostolic pioneers of our Christian faith. Read the message, glean from the message, live the message, and you will truly encounter a fruitful and blessed life.

REBECCA GREENWOOD
President and Cofounder, Christian
Harvest International
Strategic Prayer Apostolic Network
International Freedom Group

6 SECRETS TO LIVING A

FRUITFUL
LIFE

DESTINY IMAGE BOOKS BY
C. PETER WAGNER

6 SECRETS TO LIVING A

FRUITFUL

L I F E

WISDOM FOR THRIVING IN LIFE

THE FINAL MESSAGE OF

C. PETER WAGNER

WITH DORIS WAGNER

DESTINY IMAGE® PUBLISHERS, INC.

P.O. Box 310, Shippensburg, PA 17257-0310

"Promoting Inspired Lives."

This book and all other Destiny Image and Destiny Image Fiction books are available at Christian bookstores and distributors worldwide.

Cover design by: Eileen Rockwell
Interior design by Terry Clifton

For more information on foreign distributors, call 717-532-3040.

Reach us on the Internet: www.destinyimage.com.

ISBN 13 TP: 978-0-7684-5886-2
ISBN 13 eBook: 978-0-7684-5887-9
ISBN 13 HC: 978-0-7684-5889-3
ISBN 13 LP: 978-0-7684-5888-6

For Worldwide Distribution, Printed in the U.S.A.
1 2 3 4 5 6 7 8 / 25 24 23 22 21

DEDICATION

This book is lovingly dedicated to the four persons closest to me who shared life's journey with me and made my life blissfully happy, fulfilled, and adventurous:

My wonderful husband of 66 years:

C. Peter Wagner

And our precious girls:

Karen Wagner Potter

Ruth Lynn Irons

Rebecca Wagner Sytsema

CONTENTS

FOREWORD

Dr. C. Peter Wagner was an amazing example of someone who enjoyed life and finished well. In addition to being a teacher, mentor, and friend to so many, he was one of the greatest molders of modern church history. One of Peter's favorite verses was Matthew 28:19-20:

> *Go therefore and make disciples of all the nations, baptizing them in the name of the Father and of the Son and of the Holy Spirit, teaching them to observe all things that I have commanded you; and lo, I am with you always, even to the end of the age. Amen.*

Peter's professional life could be divided into four stages, and in each he changed lives around the world. His first career was serving as a missionary to Bolivia, along with Doris, for sixteen years. His second career was teaching in the Fuller Seminary School of World Mission (now School of Intercultural Studies) for thirty years. His third career was founding and developing Global Harvest Ministries. During this time he served as the A.D. 2000 United Prayer Track Coordinator. He also founded Wagner Leadership Institute for equipping and training Christian workers worldwide. His fourth career began at age 80 as the vice president and ambassadorial apostle of Global Spheres, Inc. (GSI).

Peter traveled extensively throughout the United States and other nations helping equip believers to minister in the areas of apostolic ministries, wealth, Kingdom advancement, and reformation of society. He was a masterful convener of leaders in the quest to communicate the paradigm shifts needed in the Church. As a vehicle for his teaching and equipping ministry, he penned more than seventy books during his lifetime.

This is Peter's final, posthumous book. Some people live on like those in the "faith" chapter of Hebrews 11. I've always felt that God was adding to that chapter with saints who continued on in the faith. Peter Wagner is now in the great cloud of witnesses, but part of the continuing faith chapter. This book, *6 Secrets to Living a Fruitful Life,* is a must to complete your library.

Peter was one who completed everything he began. The last day I visited with him, I said, "There are three things that you have not seen in your life: the transference of wealth into God's Kingdom purposes, the great harvest of souls that God showed you, and Doris and your family continuing on and being cared for." Just as Abraham didn't fully see some things, Peter lacked seeing these three things. I could tell he didn't want to let go until he was assured that those things would be accomplished.

Without Doris, along with Peter Roselle, this final book of Peter's would not have been finished. One thing I want you to know as you read this book is that Peter was a pioneer—not afraid to make mistakes—but always determined to prosper. Doris is the backbone of Peter's illustrious ministry. She is gifted with discernment, is an incredible mother, and most of all, is a wonderful friend. She, too, is part of that ongoing faith chapter of Hebrews 11. I am honored to be one of their sons.

I recently had a dream where we were having a huge rally. Peter was involved and running it, but I had to administrate it. He wanted "The Star-Spangled Banner" sung. I chose a best friend of mine to sing this song. He had an incredible voice and we had sung in a quartet together. When we went through the walk-through on a Thursday, it was so anointed we could hardly breathe. But when the time for the rally came and it was time for the performance of "The Star-Spangled Banner," my friend was nowhere to be found. He had vanished. I looked at Peter and said, "We can't do 'The Star-Spangled Banner' today." Then I woke up. This dream showed me that the Lord was developing a new platform of freedom for days ahead.

Peter has been instrumental in developing the platform on which we are now standing. Peter was a patriot, devoted to the United States of America, as well as any nation that we were called to be part of in developing their harvest. This book is the perfect finishing touch for Peter's new platform for the future to be created.

We are still watching for the great transference of wealth into the Kingdom to proceed, with the nations being harvested. Without understanding the revelation that the Lord imparted to Peter, I'm not sure we could connect and complete that in our generation in history. *6 Secrets to Living a Fruitful Life* is a guide to help us understand the prosperity ahead and the harvest that God is calling us to. Peter's great platform continues. This is a valuable building block to build our corporate future, and yours personally.

Dr. Chuck D. Pierce
President, Glory of Zion International Ministries
President, Global Spheres, Inc.

FOREWORD

My husband, Mike, and I first met Peter and Doris Wagner in 1989. Our lives would be forever changed with that friendship that evolved into a family relationship through years of interaction. When we met I was 38 years old and never in my wildest dreams would I have ever imagined that I would one day be writing the Foreword for one of Peter's books. He was, and will forever be, a legend. I will never cease to be amazed at the depth of what he wrote, nor the simplicity with which he presented his revelation.

When C. Peter Wagner had a conversation with you, he always made you feel like you were the most important person in the room at that moment. His writing grips a person in the same way. You become part of the truth he had discovered and share in the joy and experience of finding out something new and exciting that would change your life.

This book, *6 Secrets to Living a Fruitful Life,* was his last conversation with us in written form. It simply contains a culmination of things he had learned and wanted to leave with all those who either knew him, or would come to know him through his writing. Even though I had personally discussed some of these lessons with him, there is so much more he shared here that I found myself often thinking, "Oh, I wish I had known this kernel of truth when I was going through such and such trial or situation."

Peter was always a learner and a gleaner. These truths are, no doubt, the result of thousands of hours of study and conversations with other respected leaders. When we first met Peter and Doris, Peter was a professor at Fuller Theological Seminary in Pasadena, California. Doris was his accomplished secretary, confidant, and basically kept his life in order. She knew who to let into his office, and who to keep out. They were one of those "made in Heaven" couples. For this reason, there is no better person in the world to take what was a "work-in-progress" book, and finish the chapters that he had not quite finished, take his notes, and write what he would have wanted.

Looking at the manuscript version of the book, it noted that he started writing it July 16, 2015, and last had revised it on April 15, 2016. Peter passed away on October 21, 2016. Even though he was struggling with heart-related issues, his writing is clear and sharp.

Basically, you are holding in your hands a treasure! As you read chapter after chapter, you will live truths from his life with him. These pages are who he was and what shines through is a man after God's heart.

Chapter 1 is aptly titled, "Live in the Presence of God," and it is foundational. I didn't say to be skipped over, but that which simply will give you the "solid rock to stand on" truths. I love what he says when he declares, "The Christian life is not off and on." He goes on to tell us that he has gone through many trials and arduous difficulties; however, in each God gave him a way through. Maybe you are going through some tough times. You will gather truth from this book that will strengthen you as you come through to victory. This reminds me of the old adage, "When going through hell, don't stop!"

I particularly love the chapter titled, "Choose Your Battles." Peter proceeds to unpack various mountains that he felt he should stand on, and others that were simply not pragmatically worth wasting your emotional energy on trying to win. That is good, solid, fatherly advice! This same tone flows through in his chapter, "Dull Your Sharp Tongue." I know that part of Peter's daily prayers were that he would not have a sharp tongue. Because of his large intellect, he could quickly demolish a person with his tongue! As I knew him through the years, this was something that he admitted he worked on throughout his life. He was very honest in recognizing this and was convicted of God that it was not righteous to use his knowledge to answer his critics. One time, I remember a magazine in which the front part was taking him to task over his teaching on church growth, and the second, on the issue of spiritual warfare. He just laughed about it, and said, "Well, did they spell my name right?" I would remark back at those times, "I think I need to grow up more!"

One area that many fail to reach is the issue of convergence as either a person or a leader. Peter freely quotes J. Robert (Bobby) Clinton, his former colleague at Fuller Seminary, who is, I feel, the premier writer on this subject. Since Peter lived this message and did it well to the end, he could aptly write on convergence. There were various admonitions when I was veering away from my focus; and although at times his advice pained me, he was right. We all need to learn to "stay in our lane."

The book ends with Peter Roselle—a son-in-the-Lord to Peter Wagner—amplifying on his theme of a strong financial finish.

C. Peter Wagner ended well. He often quoted, "There is no success without a successor." He took his own, good advice, and handed off various parts of his ministry, with Doris' approval, to various members of his spiritual family.

He fought the good fight, and now has gone to the reward laid up for him in Heaven. If you follow the advice in these pages, you will too!

God bless you!

CINDY JACOBS
Ovilla, Texas

SPECIAL
INTRODUCTION

Peter and I had a marriage most people only dream of. True, we were married when he was only 20 and I was just 18, but we knew that we were madly in love, we wanted to serve God together, and we were in God's will. God blessed us with three wonderful girls and our family has always been close. Our girls adored their father, and he was always fun to live with. We have been all around the world together and loved every minute of it.

We chose to give our lives to serve the Lord on the mission field early on as new believers. We loved our sixteen years in South America as missionaries. Peter and I always worked together as a team throughout our ministry and teaching days. We then served thirty years when Peter was a professor of Strategy of Missions, Church Growth, and numerous other subjects while also serving on the Lausanne Committee for World Evangelization and later on leading the prayer movement with the A.D. 2000 organization, traveling to many nations worldwide.

Peter started Wagner Leadership Institute, which later became Wagner University. He, along with other carefully selected practitioners, traveled widely teaching the practical subjects not ordinarily available in Bible colleges and seminaries. He pioneered writings on the subjects of church growth, spiritual gifts, divine healing, prayer, spiritual warfare, deliverance, the apostolic and prophetic.

Peter had 74 published books at the time of his death. He became ill during one of his favorite assignments, teaching pastors and Christian workers in Korea. He subsequently suffered with heart failure for three years and underwent multiple heart and lung surgeries, but lost his battle in October 2016.

Since we had spent most of our waking hours together, when both of us were not traveling on ministry assignments, working and enjoying life. When I became a widow, it hit me very hard. My grief was profound, and for more than two years I struggled numbly along in daily life, but felt like half of me had been torn away. Peter once even called us "Siamese Twins," we were constantly so very close, always working together—never fought, after our few half dozen skirmishes in our first years of marriage.

When Peter died, we had been married 66 years and 6 days. He died in his favorite spot in the world. We had moved our twin beds into his home office and he was surrounded by his library, all his files, some very special farming tools, photos, and mementos of his choosing. I slept by his side, often holding his hand as he asked me to do. He slowly became quiet and unresponsive.

Our registered nurse daughter, Karen, who was named in his medical directive, said it was time to turn off the oxygen, which daughter Ruth did. He exhaled a little sigh and his heart stopped beating. He did not seem to be in pain or to be suffering. It was all so peaceful. His time had run out.

A couple of days before, Cindy Jacobs, our dear friend, said she saw a very tall angel in the corner of the office by his desk. I said I couldn't see anything, but she answered me, "That's my job." The angel was probably hanging around, getting ready to accompany Peter home, is my guess.

Some months earlier, he had begun to write the little book you hold in your hands, but died before he could finish the theme of the six most important things he learned in life, and how to die well.

It took me four years to be able to pick up what he started and put down in writing what his outlines and lectures had prepared. My writing cannot begin to compare with his, but the bare-bones thoughts are here and the message he wanted to expound on is here—bare-bones. I am sure he had numerous illustrations in his brilliant mind, and his illustrative writing stopped partway through—at least book #75 is finished, although a little late.

But, Peter, your other half got the assignment done, finally.

Doris M. Wagner
Argyle, Texas
March 2021

Introduction

REASONS FOR THIS BOOK

I now find myself in the very enviable development Phase VI, "Afterglow," of the leadership timeline developed by J. Robert "Bobby" Clinton. Clinton, for decades Professor of Leadership at Fuller Theological Seminary, has provided us with one of most informative and motivational textbooks in the field, *The Making of a Leader.*

Development Phases

I highly recommend this book to anyone who is a leader and to those aspiring to leadership of any kind. However, for those who might not get around to ordering the book right now, let me briefly refer to Clinton's timeline. Here is the way he puts it:

A development phase is a unit of time in a person's life. We identify different units by the nature of the development in a leader's life. These significant units of time are labeled Sovereign Foundations, Inner-Life Growth, Ministry Maturing, Life Maturing, Convergence, and Afterglow.[1]

Every one of these life phases is interesting and apropos, however here I am going to mention only the last two: Convergence and Afterglow. I was fortunate enough to enter my personal phase of Convergence toward the earlier end of the spectrum, namely when I was around 48 years of age. Most leaders who do get to Convergence enter it later in their 50s. This enabled me to spend a bit over thirty years ministering in Convergence, by far the most fruitful period of my life. I consider convergence so important that it appears as one of the *Six Secrets* in this book. You will find that the title of Chapter 4 is "Pursue Convergence."

Afterglow

Until then, please allow me to reflect a bit on Afterglow. If Convergence was the most fruitful phase of my leadership development, Afterglow turns out to be the most comfortable. Look at how Bobby Clinton describes this:

> For a very few, there is phase VI, Afterglow. ...The fruit of a lifetime of ministry and growth culminates in an era of recognition and indirect influence at broad levels. Leaders in Afterglow have built up a lifetime of contacts and continue to exert influence in these relationships. Others will seek them out because of their consistent track record in following God. Their storehouse of wisdom gathered over a lifetime of leadership will continue to bless and benefit many.[2]

Although some might well consider this immodest, I want to be transparent enough to say that Clinton's description of Afterglow fits quite accurately what I have been experiencing over the past few years.

I mentioned that Afterglow is the most comfortable point on the whole timeline. Why would this be? Here is what Clinton says: "There is no recognizable development task in [Afterglow] other than to allow a lifetime of ministry to reflect the glory of God and to honor His faithfulness over a lifetime of emergence."[3] Does this sound comfortable, or what? I'll take it!

Let me hasten to add that what I have just said is not to be taken as an open invitation to retirement. Afterglow does not equal retirement. I expand on my thoughts regarding retirement in Chapter 6, "Plan to Finish Well," so I will not elaborate much here. However, just for the record, at this writing I have not retired.

A Boundary Event

The year 2010 turned out to be one of the most significant years of my ministry. It was the year in which I celebrated my 80th birthday. Up until then I had never permitted a birthday party except for some low-key gatherings with the immediate family. However, in 2010 some very close friends joined forces and persuaded me to break tradition and allow my first public birthday party. I was dumbfounded by its rapid escalation. Before I knew it, Chuck Pierce had scheduled a day-long bash at his megachurch in Corinth (Dallas), Texas; and Ché Ahn did likewise at his megachurch in Pasadena, California. I had a wonderful time at both, and in hindsight I can see that this birthday was the boundary event between Convergence and Afterglow.

"Boundary event" is another Clinton term. He says that development phases are characterized by "specific boundary events."[4] They are "process items that happen during a boundary time and are instrumental in bringing about the shift from one phase to the next. ...They mark the end and then the beginning of a significant time in a leader's life."[5] When these birthday parties came, I knew intuitively that they marked a boundary event. Combined with a number of substantial life incidents, I decided to pass on to my spiritual sons and daughters all the ministries I had been leading up until then. I will give some details of this later on in the book. From that point on, however, I became one of the few (according to Bobby Clinton) to reach Afterglow. I can only thank God for the privilege.

Goodbye to Deadlines

One of the most agreeable features of Afterglow, at least to me, is the virtual absence of deadlines. For all of my life beginning when I was a kid milking cows, I popped out of bed morning after morning to the relentless bell of an alarm clock. For most of my life, year round, I was normally up at 5 o'clock in the morning because there was so much to do that day. Now I hardly ever set my alarm (at least when I am at home—participating in conferences is something else), and I get up whenever it's convenient. Not that I don't have plenty to do the rest of the day, but no one is standing over me with the whip of a deadline anymore.

In fact, when I finished writing my last book, for the first time that I could remember I did not have another book in mind to begin writing. It took me about 18 months to decide to begin writing this one, and I am only on the Introduction. How long will it take me to finish? I don't know, and I really am not that concerned.

After all, how many books are you supposed to write? At this point I have published 74, and there are a lot of bloggers on the Internet right now who wish I would have stopped writing long ago. But the books don't seem to go away. I keep hearing about new versions being published, and about new translations in other languages.

Remember that in Afterglow, Clinton said that "others will seek them out"? Well, this has been happening like it never did before. No matter where I travel, domestically and internationally, strangers come up to me and tell me how my books have helped change their lives for the good. This even happens Sunday mornings in our church, Global Spheres Center, which is connected with more than 180 nations, where people consistently make me believe that getting a photo with me is like getting one with Billy Graham! While I don't believe everything everybody says, I must say that it is fun hearing them say it. Only in Afterglow!

My wife, Doris, and I have discovered that there is another apparent upgrade to people seeking us out. Neither of us happens to be blessed with the gift of hospitality. On the Littauer personality profile, together we score near to zero as "sanguine." Nevertheless, we now find that a number of those seeking us out actually want to spend time with us in our home. We regret that our health now limits the clock time we can afford to spend interacting with guests. Even so, some are willing to travel distances, even internationally, just to be with us one on one. When this happens it is not really possible for us to say, "No—we'll be at home but we prefer to be alone!" So we have been opening our home, and we must admit that once the people are here we enjoy a good time and we're glad they came.

We've learned that we can even minister to our guests. Although we have no special skills in the area of counseling, we frequently receive emails from those who come telling how much their time with us has meant to them personally and also to their ministry. We began keeping a private list of those who have visited, and at this writing there have been thirty-five.

The Fourth Career

I mentioned a while ago that I am not retired. Instead I see myself in what I like to call my "fourth career." In 2010 I wrote an 18-page booklet that I titled *The Fourth Career: Launching into the Future at Eighty,* and I circulated it at my birthday parties. My first career was a field missionary to Bolivia (South America), my second career was a professor in the Fuller Seminary School of World Mission (Pasadena, California), and my third career was president of Global Harvest Ministries (Colorado Springs, Colorado). Now in my fourth career I serve as vice president of Global Spheres, Inc., under President Chuck Pierce in Corinth, the Dallas area of Texas.

Since I'm in Afterglow, I even get to write my own job description, which I did in the booklet. I sensed that God had given me six specific assignments to keep before me:

1. **Informing**. God has given me gifts to hear some of the things that the Spirit is saying to the churches and to communicate them to the broader Body of Christ.

2. **Imparting.** Passing on positive spiritual characteristics to those who have chosen to follow my apostolic leadership.

3. **Activating.** Helping believers discover and activate the spiritual gifts that God has chosen to give them.

4. **Empowering.** Showing believers how to be filled with the power of the Holy Spirit in order to fulfill the destiny that God has for them in one or more of the Seven Mountains that mold society.

5. **Equipping.** Urging all leaders with whom I am in contact to establish biblical alignment (equipping = *katartizo* = alignment) with apostles and prophets.

6. **Encouraging.** Helping to motivate and stimulate others to prosper in whatever purpose God has for them in this life.

I will have more to say about Afterglow in Chapter 6, "Plan to Finish Well."

My Credentials

It could go without saying that an indispensable qualification for writing a book on a fruitful life is to have had, through the years, a fruitful life. Of course God is the ultimate judge of this, but He does endow each of us with enough self-awareness to evaluate whether what we do, day in and day out, actually produces the expected results. Although it is very important in itself, I am not referring here to fruitfulness as the individual reflection of the fruit of the Holy Spirit. That is material for a different book. In this book I am talking about what we do. I am talking about using the spiritual gifts that God has given us to produce fruit thirty-, sixty-, and one hundredfold.

Humility is part of this process. Unfortunately, some have used their idea of humility as a cop-out from recognizing the fruit (or lack of it) in their lives. Even when they do produce fruit they feel that to admit they have done it would violate humility. That is false humility. They go on to say, "I did not do it; God did it." That is not right. Think about it. They actually did do it but only with the power and ability that God gave them.

God is not pleased with puppets. He created real people in His image. I have never been able to track with those who say, "God is much more interested in who I am than what I do." How you can separate the two is beyond me. They go together.

True humility is described in Romans 12:3. Here the Bible says that we should not think of ourselves more highly that we ought to think. If we do this we definitely violate humility. But what is the alternative? Please look at the answer to this question carefully. A lot of Bible readers skip over this too rapidly. The proper way to think is *"to think soberly,"* in other words to come to a realistic self-evaluation of who you are. And this sober thinking is supposed to be done *"as God has dealt to each one a measure of faith."* This *"measure of faith"* here in context, refers to the spiritual gifts that God has chosen to give you, because Paul immediately explains that we are all one body and that the members of the body do not all have the same function.

Since we all have *"gifts differing according to the grace that is given to us, let us use them"* (Romans 12:6). You use your gifts and I will use mine. The fruit from your gifts will be different from mine. Each of us will have our successes as well as our failures. Evaluating them honestly and accurately involves true humility.

Spiritual gifts will be a frequent theme throughout this book. In my opinion, understanding gifts and activating them is one of the most important principles for sustaining a fruitful life.

And by the way, if you are interested, I have a whole book published by Baker with the title *Humility*.

But back to my credentials for writing this book. I have enjoyed more years than many in thinking soberly of myself, and my life, by and large, has been fruitful. Having said this, let me add two important disclaimers:

- **I am not perfect**. I have my weaknesses as well as my strengths. I have my defeats as well as my victories. I have my blunders as well as my successes. Having said this, I am aware of several Scriptures that admonish us to be *"perfect"* like Colossians 1:28 says, *"that we may present every man perfect in Christ Jesus."* However, this word *perfect* does not mean without flaw as we usually think of it. It means maturing into the type of person God meant you to be. I think that I might be considered "perfect" in this sense, but clearly not in the sense that I never make mistakes.

- **I am not Number One**. My ministry has produced a reasonable amount of fruit in a number of areas, but in all of them there were others whose similar efforts were producing more fruit than mine. I was always glad for this because it provided role models from whom I could learn and thus have a more fruitful life.

When I first started this project, I sat down with a legal pad and began writing down some principles I had been following on the road to a fruitful life. To my surprise, I practically filled the page. That began the interesting process of reducing the list to a manageable size. First, some of my items were trivial so I crossed them out. Then quite a few could be combined, and that reduced the list. Finally I decided that six would be a good number, so the challenge was to decide which six were the most crucial. Those six principles now form the chapters in the book.

I know you will enjoy reading about them; and as you learn to incorporate these principles into your life, I dare to believe that, with God's help, you will be seeing more fruit in your ministry, whatever it may be.

Notes

1. J. Robert Clinton, *The Making of a Leader: Recognizing the Lessons and Stages of Leadership Development,* Second Edition (Colorado Springs, CO: NavPress, 2012), 37.
2. Ibid., 40.
3. Ibid.
4. Ibid.
5. Ibid., 41-42.

1

LIVE IN THE
PRESENCE OF GOD

I imagine that just about everyone who begins reading this chapter will be quite familiar with the phrase "the presence of God." Different ones may explain its meaning in different ways. In the charismatic/Pentecostal circles where I move these days, we regularly hear about "the presence of God" from the pulpit. It most frequently comes when, for whatever reason, the audience enjoys an uplifting emotional experience. The pastor may say words to the effect, "Did you feel that? The presence of God is here!" We all agree and we take it as a stamp of God's approval on what we are doing. This is just a guess, but I imagine we see this in around 75 percent of our meetings.

I bring this up simply to say that this is *not* what I mean by the secret, or guideline, "Live in the presence of God." I'm not talking about experiencing the presence of God once a week in church services—I mean 24/7. I realize that this can cause confusion. As I think back, I can hardly remember a whole sermon analyzing what is meant biblically as "the presence of God." So I felt it might be helpful to express some thoughts I have on the matter at the beginning of this chapter.

The Big Picture

First of all, let's try to see the big picture. As I have studied this, discussed it with others, and experienced the presence of God personally, I have concluded that we are dealing with three discernable levels of the presence of God:[1]

1. *Omnipresence:* God is everywhere.
2. *Indwelling presence:* God dwells in believers.
3. *Manifest presence:* God, from time to time, makes His presence unusually evident to our eyes or our ears or our spirits.

Let's take a brief look at #1 and #3 just to complete the big picture.

1. Omnipresence

Classic theology teaches that God is omniscient, omnipotent, and omnipresent. Look at that prefect "omni" in each one. This comes from the Latin meaning "all." So God is "all knowing" and "all powerful" and "all present." God is present everywhere and at all times. This involves the whole universe, which, of course, He created. God is just as much present on Mars as He is in Memphis. In fact, what do you think would be about the last place where most people would expect to find God? Probably it would be in hell. But look what Psalm 139:8 says: *"If I ascend into heaven, You are there."* Yes, everyone would expect that God would be in Heaven, but here is the surprise in the second part of the verse: *"If I make my bed in hell, behold, You are there."*

The theological omnipresence of God is true, but it is really rather abstract. For most people it is a vague concept. In fact, a lot of people think that God lives in some distant place and that He is not around here with us. These are good subjects for tea-time conversations.

3. God's Manifest Presence

God's manifest presence means that God chooses to display His glory from time to time in an obvious, notable way. It is not vague like omnipresence—it is tangible, frequently to more than one person at the same time. When preachers, especially charismatics and Pentecostals, declare, "The presence of God is here!" they mean the manifest presence. They frequently interpret it as a badge of success. For example:

- "The presence of God came with signs and wonders!" It was a successful meeting.

- "Our prayer meeting was small, but the powerful presence of God was there with us!" It was a successful meeting.

- During the sermon: "Do you feel the presence of God?" It was a successful sermon.

Without questioning the validity of statements such as those because the manifest presence of God is very important, let's analyze them a bit. "Do you feel the presence of God?" implies that a few minutes previously God was *not* present. Or even when the sermon first began, God was not yet present. Or when you were still home before you came to the church gathering you were not in the presence of God. It could also be implying that during the week you probably will not feel the presence of God, so come to church next Sunday and you will feel it again.

Now, where does this coming and going of the manifest presence of God come from? It is a carryover from the Old Testament. Before Jesus came and the Holy Spirit descended, the presence of God was located in the ark of Moses or in the tabernacle or in the temple. One of the best illustrations of this occurs in the house of Obed-Edom. David was moving the ark into Jerusalem when his journey became interrupted. *"So David would not move the ark with him into the City of David, but took it aside into the house of Obed-Edom the Gittite"* (1 Chronicles 13:13). It is interesting that the ark, where the manifest presence of God abided in those days, would be entrusted to a Gentile.

And what happened? *"The ark of God remained with the family of Obed-Edom in his house three months. And the Lord blessed the house of Obed-Edom and all that he had"* (1 Chronicles 1:14). If you read the context you will find that Obed-Edom made a fortune in those three months of having the presence of God in his house. Who wouldn't want that? That's why we often pray for the manifest presence of God in our family gatherings and in our church services.

As I was writing about this, I couldn't help but think about the song that I have sung many times: "Surely the Presence of the Lord Is in This Place." When you think about it, the presence of God surely is with us who are in this particular place, almost always implying a church building. But it is not necessarily found in other places. It goes on to say, "I can feel His mighty power and His grace." The manifest power is often tangible, not just spiritual. "I can hear the brush of angel wings!" Hearing is one of our five senses, so when this happens there is no question about the presence of God.

There is so much about God's manifest presence (#3) and God's omnipresence (#1). Whole books can be written about each of them. I included them here just to get the big picture, but this chapter is not about either one. This chapter is about *God's indwelling presence* (#2).

2. God's Indwelling Presence

God is omnipresent and we worship Him for it. God visits us with His manifold presence and we enjoy it. But we live, day in and day out, in His indwelling presence. This provides us strength and nurture in our Christian walk. It is my strategic guideline. The indwelling presence of God will be there, but it is our responsibility to make sure we are living in it.

Why do we call this "indwelling"? Because it is inside us. We're not just vaguely aware of it. We don't seek it out in a certain place. It is actually part of who we are, like our muscles or our brain.

When Does the Presence Come?

Not everyone enjoys the indwelling presence of God. It is given only to those who are born again and who have become part of God's family. Every human being is born once, but that alone does not impart the indwelling presence. It only comes if and when you establish a personal relationship with God through Jesus Christ, in other words, being born twice. I imagine that all of my readers would be born again; but just in case you happen to be one who is not or even one who has doubts, waste no time in seeking out someone who can help you pray what we call the sinner's prayer.

A Quick Test

Why not take a quick test? Which one of the following two statements would generally characterize your life?

- I expect God to walk with me on my own paths and to come around whenever I call Him.
- I want to walk with God on the paths He has chosen.

There is a big difference between the two. If you chose the first one, it implies that you are using God. That is not so good. It won't work for a fruitful life. If you chose the second, it implies that you want God to use you. That is what I have in mind for this secret, or guideline: *Live in the Presence of God.*

Let me show you two Scriptures that help us see how deep the indwelling presence of God can go in our lives:

> *God willed to make known what are the riches of the glory of this mystery among the Gentiles: which is Christ in you, the hope of glory* (Colossians 1:27).

The apostle Paul says,

> *I have been crucified with Christ; it is no longer I who live, but Christ lives in me; and the life which I now live in the flesh I live by faith in the Son of God who loved me and gave Himself for me* (Galatians 2:20).

When you think of this it is quite amazing. Jesus Christ, the Second Person of the Trinity, is actually in us. We are mere humans, but God indwells us. It is one of the greatest privileges imaginable. And Paul has taken it to a place that all of us ought to strive for—he has allowed Christ to live his life for him. Did Paul have a fruitful life? He certainly did, and this is one of the reasons for it.

I would probably agree, reluctantly, that few of us will duplicate Paul's accomplishment. I don't think I have been among those who have. However, with the exception of a few times that I have fallen short, I have never forgotten about the indwelling presence of God in my life, and this has helped me sustain whatever I might have attained as a fruitful life. That's why I list the presence of God as the first secret.

Notice that I wrote, "I have never forgotten." This does not reflect God's initiative, it reflects mine. God's initiative is to endow us with His indwelling presence, but it is our initiative to live it. That's why I call this secret, or guideline, ***Live*** *in the Presence of God.* Can we forget that God is present? Yes, I've already admitted that I have fallen short from time to time. We can forget God's presence, we can deny

God's presence, we can neglect God's presence, we can even violate God's presence. But if we do so, we suffer the consequences and we can't blame God for them. We can only blame ourselves. Why be so stupid?

Let's say everyone agrees that we should live in the presence of God. I hope this is the case by now. All you have to do as a starter is to think about praying. When can we pray? Anytime. We believe that God is here and that He listens whenever we speak to Him. Where can we pray? Anyplace we happen to be. We don't have to go to a special place like a temple to pray. We can pray with a loud voice or with no voice attached at all. This could only be true if God were with us all the time. He doesn't come and go. He indwells.

There are many other advantages if you agree with the indwelling presence of God. I would like to move on by pointing out three benefits that have been especially meaningful to me.

1. The Joy of the Lord

The Christian life is not so bad. In fact it is much better than any other kind of life you could mention. It is characterized by the joy of the Lord. If you are a believer, no matter where you happen to be

40

in your personal life, you have underlying joy. For a starter, you know that you are saved. You are no longer in doubt about Heaven or hell. When you are sure that your final destiny is Heaven, it is a cause for great joy.

Look at what the Bible says, *"You will show me the path of life; in Your presence is fullness of joy..."* (Psalm 16:11). According to this, joy is directly tied to the presence of God. If the indwelling presence is there continually, so is the joy of the Lord.

The Christian life is not off and on. If you are a true believer, it is always on. But we all must admit that the Christian life does have its ups and its downs. I like to think of them as triumphs and trials. I have gone through many trials over the years. They were really difficult, especially some of the more arduous ones. However, in each one there was a way through. There was light at the end of the tunnel. I never forgot that God was with me and the presence of the Lord brought underlying joy. So much that I have forgotten most of the trials.

A while ago a friend of mine was compiling a book and he asked me to write a chapter. I was supposed to describe the worst period of my life and then tell how I came out of it. I was interested because several dignitaries were mentioned who had already agreed to write their chapter. However, I could not remember a single period of life when I have been down. My trials could take maybe a page, but not a chapter. This brings to mind James 1:2: *"My brethren, count it all joy when you fall into various trials."* I had to ask my friend to excuse me from contributing to his book.

But I must say that my triumphs in life have greatly outnumbered my trials. The Bible doesn't have to tell us to rejoice in our triumphs because that is automatic. Triumphs bring joy and I rejoice! I can do that because I always acknowledge the presence of God. If God is present, you can enjoy your successes, and you can thank Him for them. You can tell others about them, privately and publicly. Some of my friends hesitate to do this because they feel it would be a violation of their humility. But this is not true.

I studied this and worried about it for quite a while before I wrote my book *Humility*. In it I quoted John Stott as saying, "Humility is not pretending to be other than we are, but acknowledging the truth about what we are." And then I go on to say, "We need to get rid of the notion that as soon as we recognize that we have certain strengths, we have somehow fallen into pride."[2] Denying or masking triumphs is, in fact a form of false humility because it disrespects God who gave you the gift you are using. No, rejoice in your triumphs! If you're practicing the presence of God, you will!

2. Practical Holiness

When living in the presence of God, holiness becomes second nature. It becomes almost just as much of what we do as breathing. Most of the time you breathe without thinking about it. In the presence of God holiness is just like that. You live a holy life without even trying.

Let me give you an example. I would suppose that most of us, when we were young, did some things when our mother wasn't around that we would never do when she was with us. I am referring to naughty things. We thought we could get away with it, and a good bit of the time we did. We became quite skillful at doing some things we weren't supposed to do.

Now, God is not like your mother in this respect. She would be present some of the time and absent at other times. Not God. He is present with us all of the time. He doesn't leave any wiggle room. We cannot do anything behind His back. I know that in the past I have done this or that hoping that God wouldn't notice. But I soon found that I was not getting away with it. I was displeasing God, and He knew all about it.

Let's pause and try to get the big picture regarding biblical holiness. The English word *holy* is a translation of the Greek *hagios,* which means to be set apart. Set apart from what? The answer to that question comes in two parts: positional holiness and practicing holiness. I'll explain them one at a time.

Positional Holiness

Positional holiness refers to our status as a true child of God. When we are born again, we become new creatures in Christ. The Bible says that old things are passed away and everything becomes new (see 2 Corinthians 5:17). So we are set apart from what we used to be, which in some cases was pretty bad. Our position in Christ sets us apart, in other words it makes us holy. You do not work on positional holiness if you are truly born again. It comes with the package, so to speak. God gives you the new birth and God gives you positional holiness at the same time. That is why Peter writes, *"But you are a chosen generation, a royal priesthood, a **holy nation**, His own special people, that you may proclaim* *the praises of Him who called you out of darkness into His marvelous light"* (1 Peter 2:9). All of God's people are holy because they are set apart from what the Bible calls "darkness."

Practicing Holiness

The reason I call this practicing holiness is because "practicing" implies that, unlike positional holiness, we have to work on it. It does not come automatically. Peter, whom I just quoted, also writes this to believers (who all have positional holiness), *"But as He who called you is holy, you also be holy in all your conduct"* (1 Peter 1:15). The words *"be holy"* mean that it is up to us. It is our choice. And the Bible says that our holiness is displayed by our conduct. This is a very simple statement, but I know some believers who try to get around it by insisting that positional holiness is all we need. No, our behavior counts.

Some of our behavior pleases God, and some displeases God. I'm not talking about getting into some form of legalism in defining the difference. All believers have the written Word of God as well as the indwelling presence of the Holy Spirit. We cannot do anything behind His back like many of us did with our mother.

Let's take a current example that the Bible doesn't mention specifically, but just about all of us agree that it displeases God, namely Internet pornography. I don't want to quote the percentages of Christian men and of even pastors who watch porn because they are too shocking. Most of them must be thinking that somehow God tends to overlook that behavior. If so, they are not living in the presence of God. Yes, God is always present, but we need to live accordingly: *"Be holy in all your conduct"* (1 Peter 1:15).

If we choose to live in the presence of God, I repeat, holiness becomes second nature. Internet porn and tons of other things that displease God do not enter the picture. Holiness is not a chore, it is a lifestyle! When that happens, you are "set apart" for sure.

3. You Expect Prosperity

Prosperity characterizes a fruitful life, and it comes by living in the presence of God. That's why John could write to his friend Gaius, *"Beloved, I pray that you may prosper in all things and be in health, just as your soul prospers"* (3 John 1:2).

The first thing to remember is that God wants you to be prosperous. I am appalled at Bible believers who react against this statement, which many do. Perhaps they should pay more attention to Second Corinthians 9:8 (Good News Translation): *"God is able to give you more than you need, so that you will always have all you need for yourselves and more than enough for every good cause."* We see two things here: (1) God wants us to meet our personal and family necessities; plus (2) have enough to give to others.

I am not saying that if you are a Christian you will be rich—reality disproves that. Just like, as some contend, if you are a Christian you will not be sick—reality disproves that as well. These good things will eventually come to pass, but obviously not yet. Satan, who is the god of this age, still has too much power because God's Kingdom has not fully come here on earth.

Jesus taught us to pray, *"Your kingdom come. Your will be done on earth as it is in heaven"* (Matthew 6:10). In Heaven there is no poverty and there is no sickness. This is God's will for earth as well as in Heaven. Still there are believers who are poor and believers who are sick. Let's be realistic about our understanding of satan. God created Adam to take authority and govern His creation. But satan succeeded in usurping that authority and taking charge of the world. This is why Jesus Himself called satan *"the ruler of this world"* (John 14:30). But Jesus also came as the "last Adam" in order to destroy the works of satan. He paid the price to defeat the devil on the cross. He brought the Kingdom of God. He came to reconcile the world once more to God, but He gave us the ministry of reconciliation (see 2 Corinthians 5:18).

Think of what that means. Jesus paid the *price* for reconciliation on the cross, but He is not in the business of *doing* the reconciliation. That is up to us, and for the most part we have been making progress over the last two thousand years. Jesus is waiting for us to finish. Look at what the Bible says, "[Jesus Christ] *whom heaven must receive until the times of the restoration of all things…"* (Acts 3:21). Right now Jesus is in Heaven at the right hand of the Father. How long will He be there? Until all things have been restored. Meanwhile, even though it's not God's will, we are going to have to put up with worldliness like poverty and sickness.

Four Kinds of Prosperity

Back to prosperity. Few will dispute the fact that Jesus wants the best for you in every aspect of life. Constantly living in God's indwelling presence is an important step in making this happen and bringing prosperity. I believe that God wants you to enjoy personal prosperity, social prosperity, physical prosperity, and financial prosperity. What do I mean?

1. Personal prosperity.

God wants you to feel good about yourself. When you look in the mirror, you are looking at someone beautiful. You are beautiful because you are made in the image of God. Part of God's design is that you are not supposed to look like anyone else. Others may be beautiful in their way, but only you are beautiful in your way. You love life. When you get up in the morning you have a wonderful day to look forward to. You are not worrisome or distressed. Joy and holiness, as I just explained them, are deeply ingrained. You love God because you are living in the presence of God, and that brings personal prosperity.

2. Social prosperity.

You love your friends. You have several circles of relationships, starting with those very close to you, your family, and moving out from there. Most of them are probably believers, but some might be unbelievers. I expect that most people reading this book will be church members and a strong circle of friends will be found there in the congregation. But there will be others whose strong circle of friends is in the workplace and a large part of them might be unbelievers. No matter what, you are satisfied and happy to be with friends whoever they are. The presence of God allows you to move into social prosperity.

3. Physical prosperity.

It may sound strange to bring up your physical well-being as part of prosperity. But when you think of it, it makes sense. You can't accomplish your other goals in life without having the physical strength and energy to do them. As I mentioned a couple of times before, God wants you healthy. Sure, satan is successful in invading your life with sickness and physical disabilities, sometimes for a brief period and sometimes for longer periods. But even when you are down, you need to remember the up days when you could do physically what you needed to do. I can use myself as an example of this. Right now, as I type this, I am 85 years old and very weak and fatigued, recovering from open heart surgery. But not only do I have faith that I will get my strength back some day, I also rejoice in the many years of excellent health that I have had throughout my career. I couldn't ask for more, and I attribute it to living in the presence of God.

4. Financial prosperity.

I saved financial prosperity for last because when just about anyone brings up the word *prosperity*, they are thinking financially. When you tell me that so-and-so is prosperous, you usually mean that they are rich. The Bible even says this, *"For you know the grace of our Lord Jesus Christ, that though He was rich, yet for your sakes He became poor, that **you through His poverty might become rich**"* (2 Corinthians 8:9). God wants His people, including you and me, rich. True, satan still gets in the way of this all too frequently, but the Kingdom of God is pressing him down and reducing his authority. I know some people who get upset with these ideas. They complain that it's the "prosperity gospel." But that's exactly what it is! The word *gospel* means "good news." How can anyone oppose the idea that prosperity is good news? It certainly is to most of us!

As I have studied this through many years, it has become clear to me that satan's chief tool in producing these negative reactions is the demonic spirit of poverty. This is a very powerful spirit that has invaded the church in general since around the third century. I have written a lot about it in some of my other books, so I won't elaborate much here. Just let me say that the most effective tactic that the spirit of poverty uses in the church is to get Christians, starting with Christian leaders, to believe that "poverty is piety." In other words, being poor helps you get close to God. Those who remain under the influence of this principality cannot stand the idea that God wants His people rich. Financial prosperity, in their opinion, pulls people away from God.

I need to say that I lived under the power of the spirit of poverty until I was around 50 years of age. It took three separate incidences to break it off, but I am happy to say that it no longer oppresses me. I believe that living in the presence of God was what enabled me finally to be delivered. Enough was enough! I am now financially prosperous, and I am enjoying it. I like to identify with apostle Paul who said, *"I know how to be abased, and I know how to abound"* (Philippians 4:12). This is not in the Bible, but I'll bet he wanted to go on to say, "And I prefer to abound!"

Conclusion

The first secret is to live in the indwelling presence of God. I continue to think that it is amazing that God is actually in us. When we pray, when we speak to Him, He is always there. He is never gone on a lunch break. Furthermore, living in the presence of God opens the way for joy, holiness, and prosperity. Following this guideline is a good start toward a fruitful life.

Notes

1. Robert Heidler in *The Messianic Church Arising* (Denton, TX: Glory of Zion International Ministries, 2006), 131-132. This book lists these three levels of God's presence and he adds a fourth: "God's Dwelling Presence," meaning that the manifest presence dwells in a certain place for an extended period of time.
2. C. Peter Wagner, *Humility* (Grand Rapids, MI: Chosen Books, 2002), 86.

CHOOSE YOUR BATTLES

Life is full of potential battles. This second secret to living a fruitful life is to very carefully choose the battles you want to fight.

How many potential battles have come your way? I doubt if anyone has ever counted, but I know a lot of them have. To be realistic, we have to keep in mind that different people will react to challenges for battle in different ways. Each person's personality plays a big role. I'll say more about personality in Chapter 4 on convergence, but it applies here as well. You are born with your personality. You don't control your personality any more than you control the shape of your nose. You live with it and deal with it.

If you have an aggressive personality, which some call "Type A," you will tend to choose more battles than if you have a "Type B" peaceful personality. To use the most popular personality tests, if you are a choleric (quick-tempered) on the Littauer scale, you lean more toward fighting battles than the phlegmatic (laid-back), with a spectrum in between. The same with the DISC tool: a high D is aggressive while a high S is peaceful.

I don't know of any scientific studies on this, so I'll just guess that a Type A may choose three battles a day to fight, while a more peaceful person may choose three per week. The principle of choosing which battles to fight is more needed on the aggressive side, but it applies to everyone on the spectrum. In other words, it applies to you!

It is often more difficult to choose the battles *not* to fight than to choose the battles *to fight*. One of the military principles of war is "Economy of Force." You only have at your disposal a limited quantity of combat power, whether you are fighting with spears or with machine guns. You cannot choose to deploy that power to every battle because it would dilute your strength so that you could lose every battle. You choose the battles that you can fight and win.

And keep in mind that the battles are not really ends in themselves—they are means toward the end of winning the war.

Marital Battles

To get very personal, I learned this secret a long time ago. Doris and I married in my junior year of college. I was only 20, and I needed to learn how to live in this new relationship. I had to learn by experience. Well, it turned out that during our first year of marriage we fought five battles. We had a few other skirmishes, but these five were not just disagreements but real battles—someone was going to win and someone was going to lose!

At least three of the five were over my habit of smoking cigars. Cigars made her sick. I forget what the other two battles were about, but that doesn't matter right now. You need to know that I'm a choleric and I don't mind fighting battles. I spend plenty of time trying to figure out how I can win every one. But when the year was over and I looked back on our five battles, I realized, much to my dismay, that I had lost every one!

This made me do some serious thinking. If my won-lost score for all five of our marital battles in the first year was 0-5, I perceived a pattern that I did not like. If this is the way that marital battles go, why fight them? I decided that marital battles are battles that I am no longer going to choose. And the result? In the following sixty-four years of marriage I would guess that we haven't had another five marital battles. This is a great way to live, especially since Doris is a phlegmatic who hates to fight anyway.

I have to wonder why more married couples don't try this. Divorce rates, even among born-again Christians, are sky high. I was reading an article the other day by a respected Christian journalist, whose name I won't reveal. The article was not on marriage, but here is what he wrote in passing as an illustration: "[This and that] is not unlike reconciliation in marriage. As every married person knows, reconciliation is a lifelong process requiring patience and forbearance." I had to pause and go back and read it again. Now I am one of those married persons, but for me reconciliation was not a lifelong process. It was only needed for one year out of sixty-five. How could this be? I learned the secret of choosing my battles, and I chose *not* to fight marital battles.

The main reason I stopped choosing them, of course, was that I learned through experience that I could not win. I'm a choleric. Not only do I like to fight, but I like even more to win. Sometimes, however, you may not win. I'll give you a good example of this a little later on, but first I will tell you of a battle a few years later in life that I chose *not* to fight for several reasons. I need to tell you ahead of time that the examples of battles I will describe revolve around Christian leadership, the assignment that God has given me. The principles, however, can be applied to any level of life and experience.

Speaking in Tongues

Doris and I spent the first sixteen years of professional ministry as missionaries to Bolivia. I have the gift of teaching, so my assignment was to teach in the mission's theological seminary. But I also have the gift of leadership, so after a while I became director of the mission. We had around 100 missionaries.

Our mission was strictly anti-charismatic. Tongues were not tolerated. If a missionary spoke in tongues, and some had actually done it, they were dismissed and sent home. When I joined the mission, I agreed with the policy. My seminary professors had relegated Pentecostals and charismatics to what they called "the lunatic fringe," and I was just a new Christian so I believed whatever they told me. I had no intention of ever speaking in tongues.

However, I had another set of interests. I was interested in getting the job done, fulfilling the Great Commission through missions and evangelism. As the years went by in Latin America, I couldn't help but notice that the churches and missions that seemed to be getting the job done more than anyone else were the Pentecostals and charismatics—those people who spoke in tongues. I kept quiet about this, and just tucked it away in the back of my mind.

This was in 1966. I already mentioned that I was teaching in seminary, so it wouldn't be unusual for me to be alone in my study preparing lessons. I was teaching First Corinthians and chapter 14 was next on my schedule. Now, I had taught First Corinthians a lot. In fact, I had published a book on the subject, *A Turned-On Church in an Uptight World.* I had read First Corinthians 14 numerous times. I began reading it again to get ready to teach, as I usually do. However, this time First Corinthians 14:18 seemed to jump off the page. The apostle Paul wrote, *"I thank my God I speak with tongues more than you all."* I then read this several times, in the context of what Paul was writing about, and for the first time I became impressed.

The apostle Paul was my biblical role model. I could not imagine that he was on "the lunatic fringe." And it seemed like speaking in tongues was a normal part of Paul's life. If Paul could speak in tongues, apparently whenever he wanted to, how about other people like me?

Well, I was all alone that day. No one could see me or hear what I might be saying, so I decided to go for it. I got down on my knees in a prayer position and much to my surprise I began saying words that had absolutely no meaning for me, but words that kept flowing naturally from my mouth. I was speaking in tongues! I continued for several minutes before I decided to stop. I had discovered personally what Paul was writing about!

As I began meditating on my experience, the first thing that came to mind was that I had violated the missions' rules. I've already mentioned that I was the mission director, and part of my job was to enforce the rules. But in this case I was the one! So, what to do?

Since I'm choleric, I saw a fight looming ahead. Why should a mission have a rule against speaking in tongues? We had purported to be a biblical mission, and what I had done came directly from the Bible. I began planning a fight to change the mission's rules.

Then I remembered the axiom, choose your battles! Was this a battle I wanted to fight? It would not be easy. Many of my coworkers were deeply entrenched anti-Pentecostals! They would fight hard. I thought I could eventually win the battle, but it was not a done deal. I might lose! My choice in this case, then, was not to fight the battle I had planned.

The alternative was easy. Just don't tell anyone that I had spoken in tongues. So I didn't. I kept it a secret. I never even told Doris. No one knew until around the end of the 1970s, after I had left the mission and became a member of the faculty at Fuller Theological Seminary. I wrote my book *Your Spiritual Gifts Can Help Your Church Grow*, where I mentioned tongues briefly in the Preface. It upset some people who caused me a bit of grief, but it did not become a battle. I had already chosen not to make it a battle, and I have never regretted that choice.

As I was contemplating all of this, some other thoughts entered my mind. Suppose I won the battle. Suppose I had our mission's rules changed. What would be some long-term consequences? In this case:

- Some would have left the mission and ruined their careers.
- Significant financial support would have evaporated.
- There would have been disruption in many related-mission agencies.
- It likely would not have improved the work our mission was already doing.

I am very glad that I did not choose this battle. Not only do I want to choose the battles I can win, but I want to choose the battles that ultimately count for the advance of God's Kingdom.

Keep the Right Perspectives

As you think and pray about this, be sure you keep the right perspectives. The following are a couple of them:

Spiritual perspectives.

Before you enter a battle, seek the Lord's will. Jesus said He didn't do anything unless He saw the Father doing it. If this was true for Jesus, it is doubly true for us. Take time to pray. Does God want you to choose this battle?

Personal perspectives.

Ask yourself the question: am I processing this coolly and logically or am I letting my emotions get in the way? Almost always when a potential battle looms, emotions are naturally aroused. But emotions, unsettling as they are, must not be allowed to dictate your behavior. One friend of mine was analyzing her emotional problems and she said, "I find myself looking at a situation and just knowing that I'm right and that I must go on a righteous crusade to rid the evil from those around me." Apparently her mission was to cleanse the Body of Christ of all false doctrine. False doctrine according to her interpretation. But fortunately she saw the error of her ways and corrected it. She began to choose fewer battles and she was happier for it. So were those around her.

I've told you how I chose not to fight the battle concerning speaking in tongues. I have a long list of other battles that I have refused, and I have not regretted pushing them to one side. But I also have a list—somewhat shorter—of battles that I did choose to fight, and ended up losing! These have caused me grief. Please allow me to tell you about one of them.

Signs and Wonders in Fuller Seminary

As some would know, I taught on the faculty of Fuller Theological Seminary in Pasadena, California, from 1971 until 2001. With all due respect, Fuller was the flagship seminary in the United States at the time. Actually, it was made up of three schools: School of Theology; School of World Mission; and School of Psychology. This battle was between Theology and World Mission. Psychology was not involved. I was on the faculty of World Mission.

In the beginning, namely the late 1940s, Fuller was only Theology. I graduated from there with my Master's degree in 1955. That is why it was called Fuller *Theological* Seminary. When the School of Missions came along around 1998, there was strong resentment among many of the theologians. To them theology ruled. Theology dealt with the mind. But missions? Missions was a small sub point under theology. Some thought that missions would not rank academically much higher than Sunday School. I understood them both because I had a graduate degree from each.

What was the battle I chose to fight? The battle had to do with supernatural signs and wonders including healing, miracles, deliverance from demons, and things like that. These subjects had never been taught in Theology. Let me say in passing that the School of Theology was not anti-Pentecostal; it just had never taught those things. By then I had written my book, *Look Out! The Pentecostals Are Coming,* so my position affirming Pentecostalism was public.

Things became interesting when I met Pastor John Wimber in one of my doctoral church growth classes. He thoroughly understood church growth principles, so I hired him as a church growth consultant in the Fuller Evangelistic Association, which I headed. As we were working together, he asked my permission to start a small church on weekends, which I readily gave. However, the "small" church soon became a megachurch called Anaheim Vineyard and also a good number of other churches started affiliating with John in the Vineyard Movement. Needless to say, John had to resign his position in the Fuller Evangelistic Association.

In his new church, John began teaching from Luke. Up until then, neither he nor I had anything to do with signs and wonders. But as John began to practice what he was teaching from Luke, he began to see signs and wonders in his church meetings. I was following him closely, and because of the supernatural, Anaheim Vineyard was drawing national attention. I thought that our Fuller students, both Missions and Theology, should be aware of this, so I asked John if he would help me teach a new course, "MC510 Signs, Wonders, and Church Growth." It was a course in the School of Missions, but almost immediately some of the theologians in the School of Theology began to rise up in opposition to it.

Here was the battle. Was I willing to take on the theologians and preserve MC510? I chose to fight the battle. Don't forget, I had been around the seminary just about since its beginning, and I had a degree from each of the schools. I thought I knew seminary politics very well. John taught the course for three years. It became the most popular course in the history of the seminary. But after three years, the theologians found a way to use seminary politics and ultimately have John Wimber dismissed, which automatically dissolved MC510.

Even as I write this, about thirty years later, I feel sharp pangs of disappointment. I feel I lost a very important battle that I previously thought I was going to win. And those most deprived? The students who were looking for biblical directions for their ministry.

Is Evangelism Primary?

I've given you the story of a battle I chose not to fight, then one I chose to fight but lost, now permit me to tell about a battle that I fought and won.

After World War II, a subtle shift began coming to the Body of Christ. The liberal sector always taught that evangelism could simply be present alongside the people to be reached. Preaching was okay, but not necessary. All evangelicals, of course, disagreed with this and believed that evangelism aimed at saving souls was what the Lord expected from us.

The shift I mentioned began when some very strong and outspoken international evangelical leaders began to teach that while we should preach the gospel, doing social work for the needy was equally important. I thought this was wrong so I decided to use what influence I had to oppose it. I chose this battle. I believed in the priority of evangelism.

The year 1974 saw what I consider the most important Christian gathering of the century, the

International Congress on World Evangelization held in Lausanne, Switzerland. It drew 2,300 evangelical leaders from 150 countries. A position paper called The Lausanne Covenant was drafted, and all the delegates were invited to sign it. One of the phrases in the covenant was, "In the church's mission of sacrificial service, evangelism is primary." Most of the delegates gladly signed it; but the group of leaders who thought that social service should be positioned as equal to evangelism publicly refused to sign it.

After the congress, I was asked to serve on a committee of forty-eight to move Lausanne into the future. I also was appointed to head up the Strategy Working Group that dealt with issues related to evangelism. But the battle was on! The other leaders, all of whom I knew and respected personally, continued their campaign to elevate social justice, but I and the circle of leaders I represented, all were convinced of the priority of evangelism. I'll spare recounting the numerous papers that were circulated, meetings that were held, and books that were written on the subject over the next twenty-five years. A battle? It was ferocious! But my colleagues and I were able to preserve the priority of evangelism in world missions! A battle fought and a battle won.

What to Choose

Choose your battles! The examples of applying this to real life that I have just given could be multiplied in my life, and I am sure applied to your life as well. I choose not to fight the majority of battles that come my way. That would be my advice to you as well. One of the difficulties you may encounter is that others will want you on their side in order to help them win their battles. Some of them might even be close friends. They tend to offer many enticements such as flattery or publicity or financial gain. This is where you need to be tough. The time and energy that you use to fight other peoples' battles is time and energy subtracted from yours. The operative word here is "No!" Even though it might cause some social tensions, it is worth it. Stick to your own battles.

Of the battles I do choose to fight, I end up losing a relatively small percentage. Much more frequently than not, I choose battles that I can win. Because what I have mentioned, namely that I am a choleric, this is what makes me happy. I know that others may be different. For phlegmatics, avoiding all battles at all times makes them happy. Find out where you fit and choose your battles accordingly.

Applying this principle will help you end up with a fruitful life.

3

DULL A SHARP TONGUE

Let's begin by taking a closer look at the word *dull* in the chapter title. For a lot of us this would bring to mind a knife. A dull knife is one that no longer has a sharp blade. I want to apply this to our tongue. Notice that dullness does not eliminate the knife. The handle is still there. The blade is still there. Same with the tongue. Dullness does not eliminate the tongue—it is still there. Our mind is still there and the sharper the better. Our personality is still there. Our body and body language are still there. But the tongue, the primary organ for communication, is no longer as sharp as it was. Dullness is bad for a knife, but good for the tongue.

I have often heard it said that so-and-so "is such a sweet person." This does not refer directly to the tongue, although the tongue, words that come out of the mouth, certainly enters the picture. But so do the other things I just mentioned like the mind and the personality and the body language. A sweet person, for example, usually has a twinkle in their eye. It is good to be strong and persuasive, but not by allowing the different parts of our mechanism of communication to become sharp. Try not to offend those with whom you are communicating. The Bible teaches this when it says, *"A soft answer turns away wrath, but a harsh word stirs up anger"* (Proverbs 15:1). If you can dull a sharp tongue, you are on your way to a fruitful life.

Defending Myself

I have a career as a scholar. Part of this means that I come across a certain topic that interests me and I begin to study it. I first seek out people who already know something about the topic, and I interact with them. I read books on the subject. If I can, I buy the books so I am able to underline what I consider important passages. I remember one subject I began studying that had me end up buying and reading 110 books! I organize the material and teach my content whenever I can to see how people might receive the ideas. I like it best when my audience can ask me questions. I try to take my time and not be in a hurry. Then I frequently write my own book on the subject, plus articles and blogs.

I said what I just said in order to show you how thorough I try to be before I release my ideas to the public. In my mind there should be nothing to criticize. But this has hardly ever been true. Most of the time I get tons of criticism. A lot of people disagree with me!

For example, I have a book written by another scholar that contains no fewer than 167 footnotes referring to statements of mine. And, of course, each one of them is a criticism. If you're curious enough, just Google "C. Peter Wagner heresy" or "C. Peter Wagner spiritual warfare" "or C. Peter Wagner New Apostolic Reformation," or many more that I won't bother mentioning. It's hard to believe that so many people don't like me! I felt I had to defend myself, and as a result I developed a very sharp tongue. I felt that I had to get even. My books were full of polemics. *Polemics* is the polite academic word for a sharp tongue. I loved to quote my critics and then prove, one way or another, that they were wrong. If they were wrong, that, of course, made me right! I felt good!

Dulling My Sharp Tongue

Obviously, I needed to change. Making yourself look good by making someone else look bad is clearly not the way to live. But I didn't see it back then. I thought that my critics should get what they deserve. At least that's the way I felt on the surface. At the same time, I knew deep down that God probably didn't like this behavior of mine very much. Then God brought two things into my life that convinced me I should change and look for a better pathway.

The first was writing my book, *Church Growth and the Whole Gospel.* In it I hoped to address the whole world, but especially those who had been criticizing me. The critics had been saying that my field of church growth had no social consciousness. They said that we taught evangelism but not improving society as a whole. This was not correct. We taught social change. However, my critics thought we did not give it the proper priority. And they had ideas as to how to bring about social change that I frankly disagreed with.

Actually, *Church Growth and the Whole Gospel* was my most scholarly book so far. I spent hours and hours researching what was needed to make my argument as strong as possible. I tore apart my critics by name. I used exact quotes from them and then proved them wrong. I was engaging in high-level polemics. I skillfully made my enemies look wrong because that presumably would make me look right. It made me feel very good. I felt like I was a kid once again winning the King of the Mountain game!

What made me feel even better, the book was published by Harper & Row. This was one of our main academic publishers at the time, and having a book published by them brought a good deal of prestige to seminary professors like me. I was riding high, and I felt a bit sorry for my critics. Until one day God interrupted me! This is the reason I have just been writing the things I have. Don't forget, this is all about dulling a sharp tongue.

As I recall, this came several weeks, maybe months, after *Church Growth and the Whole Gospel* had been published. Like I said, God interrupted me. I forget what I was actually doing at the time, maybe praying, but I do remember our short conversation. God said that He wanted to talk to me about *Church Growth and the Whole Gospel.* I was delighted that He first of all commended me for the book. This was a great relief, as you can imagine.

But then the other shoe fell, so to speak. It came in three words that I will never forget: "No more polemics!" God didn't explain this because He knew He didn't need to. Frankly, even though it was God's word to me I didn't like it one bit. I had been perfecting my polemics for years, and I didn't want to let them go. However, "No more polemics!" was for me the equivalent of the 11th Commandment. I had no choice. I must obey.

So I did! You're welcome to check it out; I no longer used polemics, in other words a sharp tongue, in any of my books or teachings after that.

A Misbehaving Doctoral Student

The second event that caused me to dull my sharp tongue came soon after what I just described. One of my duties at Fuller Seminary was to teach in the Doctor of Ministry program in which our student body consisted of practicing pastors as well as denominational and parachurch ministries officials. I enjoyed this very much and I saw no fewer than 2,500 pastors take my two-week courses in church growth. One of those doctoral students was an executive in one of America's largest denominations, a leader with whom I had been consulting for quite a while. We had become good friends.

After he graduated, my friend proceeded to take the outline from one of my lectures and use it word-for-word as the chapter titles of a new book he was writing. When I got a copy of his book, I was shocked. He had no permission from me to do this. He didn't even give any credit to me for his chapter titles. I was shocked. This was a clear and blatant case of stealing intellectual property! I felt this called for the use of a sharp tongue. I spent a good bit of time and thought in writing him a long and piercing letter, designed to make my friend feel the wrath of God for the rest of his life! After I drafted it, I gave it to my wife, Doris, to type.

Now this will require an explanation. It happened around thirty years ago. We had no cell phones or computers or Internet or email. At the time, Doris was my administrative assistant. Part of her job description was to process my correspondence. I would write all of my letters in longhand on a yellow pad. Doris would feed into her typewriter the appropriate letterhead plus the number of pieces of carbon paper necessary, and type out my letter. She would then bring me the original to sign. When I did, she folded it properly and sent it out by U.S. mail.

We were using this procedure with the letter I had written to my friend, when a strange thing happened. Doris typed the letter, then walked back into my office with a rather defiant look in her eye. She handed it to me with the words, "I'm not going to mail this!" Such a thing had never happened before. Who did she think she was? Wasn't I supposed to be the boss? However, she sat down next to my desk and started explaining to me how the letter would not really solve any problems, and at the same time it would make an enemy out of my friend. She didn't use the exact words, but she was telling me that I needed to dull my sharp tongue. I told her to give me two weeks, and much to my surprise, I found myself agreeing with her, so I tore up the letter!

That letter was never mailed, nor any letter like it. And guess what? My friend and I are still friends!

My Outlook on Criticism

As you will have surmised, this changed my whole outlook on criticism. I used to think that my critics were waving red flags in my face, but now I try to see them as waving yellow flags. Yes, they do think that I am wrong. Yes, they do use polemics against me. But I have learned to take a higher road and respect them as goodhearted people attempting to advance the Kingdom in their own way. I can't say that I read all the criticisms levied against me. However, I do try to dip into them from time to time so as to keep adequately informed. All of this helps me to maintain what I consider a much healthier attitude toward my critics. For example:

- I admire the serious study my critics give to my writings.

- I find that most of the time my critics quote me accurately. I would guess that 90 percent of the time, my critics are correct in what they think I am saying about a certain subject. They simply disagree with my conclusions. And, certainly, they have a perfect right to disagree with me on whatever they want.

- I take it as a compliment that, once my critics have read what I have written, they think it is important enough for them to sit down and write, sometimes pages, addressing my ideas. A much worse way to be treated would be to be ignored by my peers!

As I have worked with these situations over the years, I have attempted to introduce a bit of humor. Now when I get word that so-and-so has criticized me, I usually respond immediately, "Well, did they spell my name right?" This ordinarily evokes a chuckle, even from those who have heard it many times before.

What Can We Learn from This?

To the reader: Doris here picking up on what Peter was never able to finish. However, he left an outline of what was to appear in the rest of this chapter and it was very bare bones. I have heard him expound on this verbally and think I know the gist of what he was going to say.

He left a paper with three Scriptures that molded his thinking and acting on how to dull a sharp tongue:

- Proverbs 15:1: *"A soft answer turns away wrath, but a harsh word stirs up anger."*

- Proverbs 21:23: *"Whoever guards his mouth and tongue keeps his soul from troubles."*

- James 1:19-20 (NIV): *"My dear brothers and sisters, take note of this: Everyone should be quick to listen, slow to speak and slow to become angry, because human anger does not produce the righteousness that God desires."*

Then his brief outline contained five points. I personally have seen him act in an extremely gentle and generous way when it came to his critics, especially to his close friends. I have no idea how he intended to flesh these points out, but they speak volumes on their own. I can honestly say, having lived sixty-six years as his wife, and also for many of those years as a co-laborer in the work he did, and as his secretary and assistant, he was a genuine person—what you saw was what you got. He was never two-faced and was thoroughly honest.

Peter's outline read: **"This all starts in the mind. What you think is what you say."**

In the following numbered outline, everything in bold print is what I found. All other words are my (Doris') observations, or what I think Peter would have said. I am sorry no illustrations for these were attached, but remained locked up in his brilliant mind.

Five Ways to Dull a Sharp Tongue

1. Go for a win-win situation.

Never try to make yourself look good and the other person look inferior, unintelligent, or bad in any way. Elevate your opponent to the highest possible level and always speak kindly about him or her. There may be times when you simply will agree to disagree. But remain friends.

2. Avoid assigning guilt.

Don't ever resort to the "I'm right, you're wrong" argument. Discuss things calmly and coolly. No accusations. Simply differing points of view. Once again, avoid making an enemy out of a friend with a condemning statement.

3. Count the success of others as your success.

I have watched Peter demonstrate this time and time again. He delighted in connecting people to further their careers, in giving the outstanding up-and-comers a platform, in sharing his influence, in endorsing their books, in mentoring promising young thinkers and scholars. He was particularly a champion for gifted women, especially teachers, preachers, and intercessors who were so often passed over by other prominent colleagues. He opened the door for several who are well known internationally today. And he delighted in doing it.

4. Look at the other person's point of view.

Peter was a brilliant scholar. He was on debating teams all through high school, and graduated from all of his many degree programs as "summa cum laude" or "magna cum laude." But he was also a very humble person. God helped him to be humble because pride could have crept in often along the way. When Peter and John Wimber were working together, John said in my hearing that Peter was an extremely gentle and generous man. I would add to that, he was also a very humble genius. He examined all points of view carefully, and this helps one see the other person's point of view. It is extremely valuable to take the time to thoroughly understand the other person's point of view. The opponent feels like he or she has been given a thorough hearing and an opportunity to explain their argument. Another good way to stay friends.

5. Manage your anger.

I have seen Peter falsely accused of some things, but he learned to be gracious. He especially seemed to lower his voice if something got heated. God taught him this early on after becoming a Christian in 1950. So adding to that above list of "Genius, gentle, generous, humble (I couldn't find an alliterative word beginning with "g" that meant humble), he was gracious and godly. I thoroughly believe that he, like King David, was *a man after God's own heart.* He did not retaliate when treated shabbily. But we often did see God deal with injustices on Peter's behalf. He did not display anger publicly. And my guess is that would be the advice he would give on managing anger. My guess is he would advise an angry person to take it to the Lord in prayer and turn it over for God to take care of, and let go of it.

Always keep that "soft answer" in mind if the temptation of unleashing a sharp tongue arises. Do not yield to that temptation! A soft answer is pleasing to God and a key to a fruitful life.

4

PURSUE CONVERGENCE

The word *convergence* has taken on a number of nuances and applications in recent years. It means different things to different people. That is why I want to clarify, right up front, how I am using the word. I first learned about convergence, as a life principle, from J. Robert "Bobby" Clinton, as mentioned in the Introduction of this book. Bobby and I were friends and he had mentioned convergence to me from time to time, but it was greatly clarified when his book, *The Making of a Leader,* was released. In his book he sketches out what he calls the "Leadership Time-Line."

His Leadership Time-Line has five phases. I'll list them so we can see the context, but I am only going to concentrate on the last one as a secret for living a fruitful life. The phases are:

- Sovereign Foundations
- Inner-life Growth
- Ministry Maturing
- Life Maturing
- Convergence

If any of the first four interest you, just order the book from Amazon. The fifth, convergence, for many, will be the most important secret in this book. I want to go into some detail, so that is why this is one of the longer chapters.

Please keep in mind that this lesson is mainly for leaders. By this I do not mean just the highly visible leader, but right down the line. I mean all who have an influence on how others think and behave. It could be in the home. It could be out in the workplace such as in a school or in an office or on a construction job or in a corporation. Wherever you are on your journey, convergence will help you reach your destiny.

Chuck Pierce gave a prophecy a while ago. If applied correctly, it will help us focus on the process of convergence: "Do not forget that the Lord has brought us to a 'narrowing' season, and is saying:

'A new corridor is forming and I will narrow your way. You must narrow your desires. I am sanctifying desires and narrowing the corridor through which you will walk.'" Convergence usually brings a "narrowing season," like we see in the prophecy. Just keep that in mind.

I think it would be most helpful to organize my thoughts under three categories:

1. Why convergence?
2. What exactly is convergence?
3. How do we reach convergence?

Why Convergence?

You are undoubtedly asking why convergence is so important. You are probably wondering why you should make the effort to strive for convergence in your life. Let me begin by asking you a question. I know the answer you will give, but I want to make the point as clear as possible. Whenever you undertake an important task, do you want your results to be poor? ("No!") How about mediocre? ("No!") Well, how about excellent? ("Yes!")

Of course, everyone wants to be excellent in what they do. Convergence will help you be excellent more of the time! I didn't say *all* of the time, because everyone messes up occasionally whether they are in convergence or not. All I want to say is that when you reach convergence, you will exhibit more excellence than before. I can guarantee that!

To be more specific, the main reason why you should pursue convergence is that it will maximize the use of your time, your talents, and your energy. Let's take a look at this.

Your Time

I'll bet that you, more than once, have said words to the effect, "I really want to do this, but I never have the time." This indicates that you have not reached convergence. You really do have the time. You have as much time as anyone else, namely twenty-four hours per day. It's just a matter of how you choose to use your time. Convergence will help you prioritize your use of time wisely. You do have enough time to be excellent!

Your Talents

Never think that you have no talent. I lived for twenty years in Colorado and have seen a lot of snow. I have been told that no two snowflakes are exactly alike. It is the amazing creativity of God! You also are a one of a kind and as such you have talents that should not go to waste. Convergence will help you maximize your talents.

Doris here. Peter last sat at his computer and wrote the first 663 words of the beginning of Chapter 4, "Pursue Convergence," on August 24, 2016. He then became too weak and bedridden and was on hospice care at our home where he passed away to glory on October 21, less than two months later. He "finished well" before he could get down on paper all he meant to write.

I located the outlines and lectures he had been giving on the remaining topics. I will fill in the blanks as best I can from those notes so at least the bare bones content will be there and the book will be finished. I feel it has much to offer to others who can benefit from the teachings God gave to Peter. Bear in mind that I am taking the information directly from his lecture notes and PowerPoint material, so the words "I, me, my, mine, etc." refer to Peter speaking those words, not to me, Doris.

Your Energy

Your energy is limited. Make the best use of what you have. Here is a principle I am pretty sure holds true: If you are doing something you like to do, you accomplish more in the same period of time. What you *want* to do takes less energy than what you *have* to do. Convergence helps you know the difference.

What Does Convergence Look Like?

Convergence is spending most of your time doing what you are good at and doing what you are supposed to be doing. Bobby Clinton's observation concerning this appears in his book *The Making of a Leader.*

> In convergence, Phase V, God moves the leader into a role that matches his or her gift-mix and experience so that ministry is maximized. The leader uses the best he has to offer and is freed from ministry for which he is not gifted or suited.[1]

Clinton's research has shown that not many leaders reach convergence. We have definitely not taught or practiced it enough. I definitely believe that one reason is ignorance. We haven't taught or practiced it enough.

Clinton observes also:

> In the long haul, God is preparing you for convergence. He is conforming you to the

image of Christ (Romans 8:28-29), and He is giving you training and experience so that your gifts may be discovered. His goal is a Spirit-filled leader through whom the living Christ ministers, utilizing the leader's spiritual gifts.[2]

In my opinion, the lack of this teaching today is retarding our assignment to get to positions of influence in the Seven Mountains. These are the seven molders of our culture so aptly taught by our precious, brilliant friend, Lance Wallnau. They are: Religion, Family, Government, Education, Business, Arts and Entertainment, and Media. Lance advocates that we need Christians at the top of those mountains to positively influence that field for Christ.

No matter where you are in your mountain today, convergence will help you get to where you need to be tomorrow.

How Do I Go About Reaching Convergence?

Are there any practical steps I can take? Here is what Bobby Clinton has to say about that:

During Phase V, convergence occurs. That is, the leader is moved by God into a role that matches gift-mix, experience, temperament, etc. The role not only frees the leader from ministry for which there is no gift, but it also enhances and uses the best that the leader has to offer. Not many leaders experience convergence.[3]

My credentials—What right do I have to teach Clinton's Theory of Convergence?

Bobby Clinton: I knew Bobby very well, both as a student and as a colleague. Bobby came to Fuller School of World Mission after careers as:

- A captain in the Marines
- An electrical engineer
- A missionary to Jamaica

We worked together very closely for two years in the late 1970s while he was serving as my teaching assistant. Because he excelled in the subject of leadership, I was able to help encourage our faculty to hire him. He subsequently wrote his outstanding book containing these teachings concerning convergence. He later told me that he was watching me and I became his working model for convergence. I reached convergence in my late 40s and early 50s.

Lance Wallnau: Lance was the one who encouraged me to take these teachings on convergence and craft a whole lesson out of them, begin teaching the subject as opportunity arose, and so I did.

Four Steps Toward Convergence

Now, let's get down to business! How can you move toward convergence? I will suggest four helpful steps toward convergence: (1) deploy your spiritual gifts; (2) tune in to your temperament; (3) play your position; and (4) choose your battles. Let's look at each closely.

1. Deploy your spiritual gifts.

I have spent many years teaching and writing concerning this vital topic. Some of the resources I have produced include the following books *Your Spiritual Gifts Can Help Your Church Grow* (over a quarter million copies sold to date). I also wrote a more concise version of the larger, first book, called *Discover Your Spiritual Gifts,* which includes a helpful questionnaire giving clues as to which spiritual gifts may be yours. I also produced the same questionnaire in booklet form titled *Finding Your Spiritual Gifts,* which to date has sold more than a million copies.

These materials have turned out to be very helpful tools, especially for Bible group studies and discussion, Sunday School classes, and the like. They are written in such a way as to be acceptable to evangelicals and charismatics alike.

Recall Bobby Clinton's statement: "The leader's role matches his or her gift mix." So then the question becomes: "What is a gift mix?" Let's look at Scripture for further enlightenment.

God has given spiritual gifts to everyone who is born again: *"But the manifestation of the Spirit is given to each one for the profit of all"* (1 Corinthians 12:7).

God is the one who decides which gift or gifts you should have to fulfill your destiny: *"But now God has set the members, each one of them in the body just as He pleased"* (1 Corinthians 12:18).

God has given more than one gift to most believers = their "gift mix."

It is not up to you to decide which gifts you should have. It is God's decision.

In light of all of this, what should be your action? *Discover your gifts.*

Let me pass along a bit of good advice: Adopt the constitutional view of spiritual gifts, not the situational view. This begs the question, what is the difference? Let me explain.

The situational view of spiritual gifts is that of classical Pentecostals and most charismatics. Their view is that when a person is filled with the Holy Spirit, that person receives all the gifts of the Spirit. Following that, according to the situation that arises, God will activate whatever gift is needed. For example, if that person leads another to Christ, the gift of evangelist has been operative. If the same person prays for the sick and a healing occurs, the gift of healing has kicked in. When that person passes along some good advice to another, the gift of wisdom manifested. However, the situational view makes it difficult for an individual to find his or her personal gift mix and reach convergence.

The constitutional view tends to be the view of most evangelicals and some charismatics. This view holds to the assumption that God chooses which gifts to give you and they become part of who you are. So my advice to born-again believers is to concentrate on discovering, developing, and using the gifts and gift mix that you have. Do not allow yourself to minister with gifts you do not have.

Let me give you two examples: one negative example and one positive example.

The negative example is Edward John Carnell, who died in 1967 at the age of 48. Edward John Carnell was possibly the most respected theologian of his time. He taught me in my theology classes at Fuller Theological Seminary as I was studying for my Master's in Theology in the 1950s. Every student voted him the #1 teacher. He taught with no notes! Then he was appointed president of the Seminary. The next day he walked into class with notes. About ten years later he committed suicide. It is my opinion that he attempted to minister outside his gift mix.

I will use myself as the positive example. The year was 1979, eight years after I had returned from my missionary work in Bolivia and took up a teaching position at the Fuller School of World Mission. I knew that my primary spiritual gift was teaching— knowledge and leadership were also there. In 1979 Bobby Clinton was my teaching assistant.

I was teaching a full load at the Seminary, but was also running the Charles E. Fuller Institute for Evangelism and Church Growth. John Wimber was working for me—we had a national ministry consulting with denominational leaders and were conducting national conferences. I was traveling to ten countries per year.

Seminary President David Hubbard visited me and asked the question, "Would you consider becoming Dean of the School of World Mission?" The Fuller

School of World Mission was the top school of missiology in the world at the time. I immediately responded "No!" Why? I did not have the spiritual gifts.

He was astounded to hear that answer and would not accept it at first. But just a few weeks before our meeting, I had taken the PF16[4] test as a whim, and one of the results that came back stated clearly, "He should not be in academic administration." When David saw that, he understood! This probably saved both me and the School of World Mission from disaster.

It was also during this time that I discovered that the Fuller Seminary faculty meetings were boring, so I quit going. I was called in to the President and Provost's office. They wanted to know why. I asked them if they wanted me to be a cog in the educational machinery or move out to what God had called me to do? I received a letter stating that more action needed to be taken but I never heard anything more!

Remember step 1 toward convergence: *deploy your spiritual gifts.* Now, let's move on to the next step.

2. Tune in to your temperament.

Why is it important to know your temperament?

1. You understand yourself better.
2. You understand others better.

God matches our spiritual gifts to our temperament. Two of the better known personality profile tests are DISC and Littauer. Florence Littauer's work is titled "Wired That Way." They provide the tests one can take to discover his or her temperament. There is also helpful information in my book *Finding Your Spiritual Gifts*.

I discovered this about my temperament:

I scored high in:

- Choleric: (leading, organizing, action, goal-oriented)
- Melancholy: (orderly, analytical, creative, schedule-oriented)

I scored low in:

- Phlegmatic: (peaceful, agreeable, quiet, calm)
- Sanguine: (talkative, friendly, demonstrative, charming)

I used to envy phlegmatics and sanguines. Before convergence: I tried to be more like them! After convergence: I don't want to be one! Result? I am much happier being who I am!

3. *Play your position.*

What matters most? I earned three Varsity letters in my athletic days. All were in team sports: baseball, basketball, and soccer. Especially in basketball and soccer the coach would often shout "Play your position!" The coach places you on the team according to your strength. Playing your position well will help your team win. What matters most at the end of the day is not how well you play, but who wins the game.

My good friend John Maxwell has produced a number of excellent books on the topic of leadership. In his book *The 21 Irrefutable Laws of Leadership,* he makes the brilliant statement, "As a leader, you should spend most of your time working in your areas of greatest strength."[5] This seems like excellent advice.

John then goes on to discuss one of his "irrefutable laws," namely "The law of Priorities." Here he states, "Take some time to reassess your leadership priorities. Are you spread out all over the place? Or are you focused on the few things that bring the highest reward? If you aren't living by the Law of Priorities, you might be spinning your wheels."[6]

4. Choose your battles.

As you begin to move up in leadership, you will gain more influence and many others will want you to be on their side. For what? To help them win their battles! They frequently offer many enticements including flattery, publicity, and even financial gain. If that fails, some may even resort to putting you on a guilt trip.

Ask any general in the armed forces concerning the rules of warfare, and you will get the response, "Choose your battles carefully." Namely, choose the battles you can win! It then follows that if you choose some, you will reject others. The most important word in reaching convergence is "NO!" This is hard because it frequently hurts people's feelings, but it is one of the prices you pay. If you try to fight every battle that comes your way, you cannot reach convergence.

So the question naturally arises, "How does one choose which battles to fight?" Let me offer the two criteria I have found most helpful:

- The first is to seek God. You should seek God because the battles you say "No" to fighting are probably good battles, they are just not yours.

- The second is to evaluate your passion. Ask yourself the question, "Do I have a God-given passion for this battle?" If you do not find within yourself a passion for that particular battle, you will probably lose it. So, say "No!"

Conclusion

In conclusion, let me offer you six advantages of reaching convergence:

1. You will get the greatest return for the use of your time, talents, and energy.

2. The quality of your work and ministry will improve.

3. What you do will be more enjoyable.

4. You avoid the strain of attempting to do things you're not equipped to do. This can be very frustrating and burdensome because you do not enjoy it and the results are poor. I am a little envious of friends of mine who:

   - Memorize the Bible
   - Preach
   - Sing with good tune and harmony
   - Pray hours a day

- Have their own TV programs
- Take good offerings
- Do mass healings
- Minister after church service

These are all good, but none of them are part of my convergence package.

5. You are better equipped to make important decisions. Let me give you an example. In 1998 I received a prophecy that I would start a training school and call it Wagner Leadership Institute. The question immediately arose, "Should this be a pre-service or an in-service school?" That is, preparing young people for the ministry (pre-service), or teaching pastors and leaders already in ministry (in-service) how better to serve and be more fruitful. In Fuller I taught both with the in-service being more effective and enjoyable. But in 2002 I decided to try a pre-service school. It lasted only one year and we closed it down! I had stepped out of my convergence! I should have said "No" to this.

6. You will be much more able to fulfill the destiny that God has planned for you. In my 50+ years of ministry, the last half have been happier and more productive. This is probably the direction you will want to go.

Remember that convergence maximizes your use of your time, talents, and energy. Pursuing convergence will certainly lead to a more fruitful life of service to our triune God.

Notes

1. J. Robert Clinton, *The Making of a Leader: Recognizing the Lessons and Stages of Leadership Development*, Second Edition (Colorado Springs, CO: NavPress, 2012), 46.
2. Ibid., 33.
3. Ibid., 32.
4. The 16PF is a highly effective, fully rounded personality factor questionnaire revealing potential, confirming suitability, and identifying development needs.
5. John Maxwell, *The 21 Irrefutable Laws of Leadership* (Nashville, TN: Thomas Nelson, 1998), 177.
6. Ibid., 182.

5

SUCCEED THROUGH THE SUCCESS OF OTHERS

This chapter is apparently something the devil did not want to see the light of day. I, Doris, am writing this with but one page of some very sketchy notes on a yellow pad that Peter had been preparing for this chapter during his final days. I think I know what he would have said, although I fully realize that my writing skills are very poor compared to his. I do not know which illustrations he had in mind to flesh out his points, but will do the best I can.

I had this chapter completely written and thought it was what Peter would have wanted. I was actually pleased with what I had done. But, since I am pushing 88 years of age at this writing, my computer skills are wanting and I somehow managed to delete the whole thing. My computer whiz daughter, Ruth, worked hours to try to recover it, but to no avail. So I am starting over after having lost several days of very hard work with no notes of my own. I saw it was missing when I was ready to push the "print" icon to add it to the manuscript.

We think we know the cause. In late April, just as Ruth and I were preparing to leave on a month-long ministry trip to the Midwest, lightning struck our house and wiped out our automatic lawn sprinkler system and our total communication system—telephones, Wi-Fi, Internet, it fried a computer and my printer as well as a large screen television in my bedroom that Peter bought me when we moved into our new home in Texas. There were other casualties that I can't recall. But in the reinstallation of the programming on the computer system, the "automatic save" option was left out, which explains why a stupid mistake of mine was so costly. Ruth and I were both in the house at the time of the lightning strike, and survived just fine.

The theme of this chapter totally personifies Peter. John Wimber once said of Peter in my hearing that Peter was "extremely gentle and generous." No one knew Peter better than I. He was indeed gentle. After God told him there should be no more polemics in his ministry, he did an about-face and became very kind and gentle in his teaching as well as his interaction with other people.

He was indeed extremely generous. He handled the finances of the family and we practiced the "graduated tithe." Each year we tried to give a percentage point or two more of our income away to other ministries and charities. We were giving away at least 40 percent of gross earnings before taxes. On top of that, we practiced giving alms to the poor and other offerings. All of our tithe money was deposited in a separate bank account and held as sacred and for distribution only.

Since becoming a widow, I still do a double tithe of 20 percent of what comes in to me, plus offerings as I am able. Peter totally taught me to be generous, and I enjoy it. Our daughter Ruth and I volunteer to feed the poor at Thanksgiving and ring bells many days for the Salvation Army between Thanksgiving and Christmas to help feed the poor in our city. We enjoy giving back as we are able. I greatly enjoy helping stock the pantry shelves of the Salvation Army every few months, and giving gifts at Christmas to the various outreaches our church sponsors.

Peter was truly a genius, but tried hard not to wear it on his sleeve. He was honestly humble and tried to teach others that virtue. He was a brilliant, hard-working person who truly wanted to serve and please God. I so admired him for that. And he was genuine. What you saw is what you got. He never tried to impress others with his brilliance. Instead, he wrote his thoughts to share with the Body of Christ. I often heard him say, "I can't stand having an unpublished idea." I once brought to his attention something I read somewhere that to me looked like it was something original Peter had taught but did not give him credit. "That's okay," he said, "God will give me a new idea."

I have been enjoying reading through Peter's Bible. It is profusely underlined and he has written a number of notes alongside the text. As I was writing this, it just so happened that my morning reading took me to Luke, chapter 6, verse 40 that says, *"A disciple is not above his teacher, but everyone who is perfectly trained will be like his teacher."* In the margin, Peter penciled: "This is why teachers are glad when their ideas are surfaced in others." His generosity showed up again, in my estimation.

One more antidote. Peter was a man of his word—a true "promise keeper." He admired the Promise Keeper movement, but never got involved in it. He told me that he never had to renew wedding vows or past promises because he never broke the first ones. He couldn't relate to promise breakers. He never looked at another woman in lust or got involved with porn or anything of the like. Ours was a marriage most people only dream of, with great affection and true loyalty for each other—and best of all, we got to work together all of our married life. The very last words he uttered were to me, and they were, "I love you, Baby."

On with the illustration of his keeping his word. I recall that one of the few fights we had after that first year of marriage was about fifteen years later when we served as missionaries and lived in the city of Cochabamba in Bolivia. Peter was the director of the mission and I was his executive assistant. Revolutions to overthrow the government were very frequent. As a matter of fact, we discovered that Bolivia had more revolutions than years of liberation from Spain—well over 200 at the time, as I recall!

University students were often deeply involved in these uprisings. One of these revolutions was taking place during a certain week when Peter had made a commitment to deliver a teaching at the Baptist seminary across town. The only trouble was that the university stood between our home and the seminary, and Peter had to drive right through that area to get to the lecture hall. I was afraid for his life. The riled-up university students were tipping cars over and setting them on fire, and I did not particularly want to become a widow while still in my late 30s and with three children to care for.

Peter insisted on going because he said, "I have given them my word." This, to me, seemed like a lame excuse when people were being shot in the streets. I felt it too dangerous for him to go out. But Peter's "word" prevailed over my pleading with him to stay safe, and he went anyway. God did protect him, and he found a circuitous route safely there and back home. But our fight was heated. I even remember I had a red and black print dress on at the time! I don't think we fought since, or if we did, I can't remember it.

So now I will attempt to flesh out the scanty, bare-bones outline Peter left behind for Chapter 5,

"Succeeding Through the Success of Others." This is Peter's outline and mostly Peter's words. In my opinion, it is one of the greatest legacies he is leaving behind here on earth.

Let's look at the title, especially "Success of Others."

1. Success

Success is simply accomplishing a goal. You do this many times in your daily life. But I am talking about the big picture—life goals. You will have a number of them. Some will be short-term goals and others will be long-term goals.

2. Others

You will attain your goals mostly by diligence and hard work. Success is a result of your own achievement. But here is my life principle: Set as one of your chief life goals to help others achieve their own personal goals. If they are successful, guess what? You are successful! This fits in with what the Bible says in Philippians 2:4: *Let each of you look out not only for his own **interests**, but also for the **interests** of others.*

Interests = goals. It includes your own goals and the goals of others. Here is an interesting question: Which of the two is most important? We might think that *my goals* are the most important. Or that they are equally important. But here is what the Bible says in Philippians 2:3:

> *Let nothing be done through selfish ambition or conceit, but in lowliness of mind let each esteem others better than himself.*

It looks like the others' are more important!

3. Avoid selfish ambition

This also means selfishness or rivalry. It's not that we don't strive to attain our own goals. But we do not attain our goals at the expense of others. Paul admonishes us in Ephesians 4:1-6:

> *I, therefore, the prisoner of the Lord, beseech you to walk worthy of the calling with which you were called, with all lowliness and gentleness, with longsuffering, bearing one another in love, endeavoring to keep the unity of the spirit in the bond of peace. There is one body and one Spirit, just as you were called in one hope of your calling; one Lord, one faith, one baptism; one God and Father*

> *of all, who is above all, and through all, and
> in you all.*

4. Avoid conceit

This is mental. This is thinking more highly of yourself and not thinking soberly. Never get the idea that "I am number one." Embrace lowliness of mind, which some Bible versions translate as humility. Everything you do should be clothed in humility. Humility is not degrading you or your goals. It is simply putting others before yourself. A great passage of Scripture to corroborate this thought is First Peter 5:5-7:

> *...Yes, all of you be submissive to one another,
> and be clothed with humility for "God resists
> the proud, but gives grace to the humble."
> Therefore, humble yourselves under the
> mighty hand of God, that He may exalt you
> in due time, casting all your care upon Him,
> for He cares for you.*

5. Associate with winners, not losers

This is a good way to put others before yourself. When I was a teenager, I played a good bit of tennis. I thought I should win every time, so I played with people I could beat. One day my father scolded me,

"You will never be a good player if you only play with people you can beat. Always play with someone better than you." The other person won the match, but I won too. Because of the challenge I learned new skills, I tried harder. and I played better by associating with winners.

6. Help others to succeed

If you do this, they will be:

- More popular; their books will sell more, etc.

- More famous; they will make more money, etc.

- More effective

7. Do not be jealous or envious

These are poisonous emotions! Let's take a look. Jealousy is hostility toward another person perceived to have accomplishment, honor, or advantage. My advice is don't feel hostile, rather rejoice at their success. Envy is defined as a feeling of discontent or resentful longing aroused by someone else's possessions, qualities, or luck.

Doris here. Point 7 was the last note that Peter made on the yellow pad. But he did put down another little clue I think he wanted to include. It was the name of a woman who was a heavy donor to Global Harvest Ministries. This was the name we had given to our ministry of leading the A.D. 2000 Prayer Track and the Spiritual Warfare Network and Strategy Working Group it contained.

At that time we needed a substantial budget to hold our seminars on intercession, provide newsletters, print and mail information on the yet-unreached people groups in the 10/40 Window, hold occasional international meetings, pay overhead, and sustain our staff. We started out with just two of us plus volunteers, but grew to 53 employees at our largest. There were times when funds were so short that two, three, and four months in a row went by and I (Doris, the Chief Operating Officer) could not take a modest salary because there just was not enough to pay all of us. My employees never went without salary or medical insurance. Peter's other earnings had to carry us through as a family. So funds were always tight.

To get back to our lovely donor friend. She was in the clothing business and as I recall gave us $2,000 a month for a good stretch of time. But a colleague was in the beginning stages of a new and exciting ministry among young people to fast and pray and gather in large meetings. This donor decided to switch her monthly giving to that new ministry. It is a great ministry and we were in cahoots, not competition. We simply had to say, "Okay, God, provide our needs from elsewhere."

Peter and I have long since learned to thank God for what we have had in the past and let it go. As long as we are doing what He wants us to do, He will provide. It seems as though there is never excess, but enough to do His bidding and move forward.

His Gift of Influence

In conclusion, I am going to add an observation here. Peter often commented to me that God had given him a gift of "spotting winners." Often there were younger people in ministry, frequently his students, sometimes the leaders of lesser known ministries who were just starting out. He especially enjoyed giving a platform to or endorsing books or otherwise encouraging gifted women. Some were preachers or teachers, others were apostles, prophets, or intercessors, so often overlooked by others. When they had the right connections, great things got accomplished for the Kingdom. Several prominent women were given the platforms at conferences that they deserved. Intercessors were recognized as vital cogs in the wheels of evangelism, church planting, and business.

The door frequently opened for Peter to have quite an influential international ministry through the Lausanne Committee for World Evangelization, the Latin American Committee for Evangelism, the A.D. 2000 Movement and many other avenues and organizations, both large and small. He was constantly using his influence to help others move up in the ranks. Peter used every available opportunity in an attempt to coordinate groups and people in order that more be accomplished in bringing God's Kingdom to earth.

It sort of harkened back to our very early farming days when both of us used work horses in farming. Later on, during our twenty wonderful years in Colorado, we often attended the annual livestock show and rodeo in Denver held during January. We particularly loved to watch the heavy horse pull. They were usually enormous Shires or Belgian draft horses. It took great skill on the part of the driver to get those powerful animals in perfect step and harmony, but when they achieved that, the power they unlocked was astounding. The amount they could pull was not added, it was multiplied many times over. It is said that a normal draft horse can pull 4 tons. When two are harnessed together, they can pull 12 tons.

As I was looking at this on the Internet to get these figures right, I saw that a team of Shire horses recently pulled 45 tons, that's 90,000 pounds! Teamwork, determination, precision, timing, breeding, and such, plus the right driver to get them to start precisely together, and to pull equally, results in the team doing great things. In those competitions, the winning horses had to pull the load for a certain distance, somewhere around 40 to 50 feet. And these horses love to pull, which is where the phrase "straining at the bit" comes from. They can't wait for the signal to pull. So it was with teaming up the right winners for Peter. There is great anticipation in getting a tough job done well for the Lord. Peter had that gift.

His Gift of Convocation

Peter also had a very effective gift of convocation. He was able to pull together many like-minded, gifted people in specific areas of ministry to further their ministries. At the age of 80, he turned over all of them, except the inner circle of his closest friends who considered him to be their apostolic leader. That one simply had to disband; the Eagle's Vision Apostolic Team, EVAT. It was the one I enjoyed the most because it consisted of about twenty-five leaders of like minds and we gathered once a year to share victories, dreams, visions, and compare notes. They were our closest circle of friends. I miss them greatly during these days of widowhood and being confined to a wheelchair since I lost my leg two years ago.

There are several other organizations that continue on today that Peter pulled together, led for years, and then handed over to his hand-picked successors.

One of the first was the Apostolic Council of Prophetic Elders. As Peter often joked, trying to lead this group was the closest thing he ever attempted that resembled herding cats. Peter's choleric/melancholic personality and vast experience in leading organizations and committee meetings sort of flew out the window after the first ten minutes of the annual meetings. He totally lost control of things and Robert's Rules of Order were not to be seen again for the next three days. Prophets are special, wonderful people and some of our very best friends whom we loved dearly. So these meetings were unusual, but a great deal of fun watching what each was hearing from the Lord. The group is now ably being led by Cindy Jacobs and has grown greatly and expanded internationally and moves along steadily and vibrantly.

Peter also pulled together the educators into a group called the Apostolic Council for Educational Accountability. It too is moving along well today and the educators exchange ideas and share forward thinking in the field of theological education and its curricula. There are always new and exciting ways to educate God's people for the work of the ministry. The electronic age has pushed us forward rapidly, and these leaders share and encourage one another.

Both Peter and I founded the International Society of Deliverance Ministers; and now there are between 250 to 300 deliverance ministers active in this organization. We share information and methodologies concerning deliverance issues once a year. Bill and Sylvie Sudduth led that organization. Bill passed into Heaven on November 1, 2020, and Sylvie is bravely carrying on the Society of Deliverance Ministers. It is very important to me to attend these meetings every year to learn more about the pervasive diabolical problems facing humanity today. Successful practitioners in the ministry of casting out demons teach ways to set people free from satan's bondages.

Peter also helped John Kelly for about ten years lead the International Coalition of Apostles, now renamed the International Coalition of Apostolic Leaders. It has grown vigorously since Peter turned it over totally to John Kelly, when he turned 80. Peter worked very hard to help legitimize the office of apostle in today's culture. It is very international in scope and regional as well. There are now many hundreds of members. I visited the annual meeting for a day for the last two years and it is moving along very nicely. Peter would be pleased.

Peter tells about Wagner Leadership Institute (WLI) extensively in his memoirs, *Wrestling With Alligators, Prophets, and Theologians*. His dream has always been to train gifted men and women for ministry in the practical issues of theological education, with practitioners as the professors. Peter always sought out successful practitioners as professors. Also, the classes taught are, for the most part, not found in the curricula of Bible schools and seminaries. They include teaching of the apostolic, spiritual warfare, healing, and the prophetic evangelism, intercession, and other subjects needed by ministers and missionaries.

Peter was always on the cutting edge in theological education. He turned over WLI to Ché Ahn, also when he turned 80. It has had its ups and downs since its inception twenty years ago, but now Ché has named Benny Yang as the head and it has since become Wagner University. The format of classes has changed somewhat, and 80 percent of a degree can now be earned online. It has become popular internationally, with Japan our newest added country. We have students from many nations of the world, and it is moving ahead nicely at this writing.

In my observation of Peter over our many years of working together, I was always of the opinion that he was out in front of the church universal by about ten years. He was committed to hearing accurately what God was saying to His people and conveying that accurately to the Body of Christ using all the venues open to him and his influence.

Writing was a natural gift and this is his 75th book. It took about ten years for many of his ideas to catch on. Peter, like many gifted teachers, didn't have a lot of exposure to television and radio because there was no financial base, so he had to depend on the international organizations of which he was a member, seminars, his books, and just plain teaching where he worked and at the invitation of others. He taught thousands of students in Doctor of Ministry classes at Fuller seminary. He had the largest classes in the history of the seminary, by far—with the most controversial being the Signs and Wonders class that he team-taught with John Wimber.

I feel one of our greatest successes was leading the worldwide prayer movement during the decade of the 1990s. God led Peter to study intercession when he accepted the position of leading the United Prayer Track of the A.D. 2000 Movement led by Luis Bush. This was a volunteer position and he and I formed Global Harvest Ministries in order to carry out the job. We had to raise our own funds, and our mandate was to recruit prayer for the 1,739 unreached people groups of the world. These people groups were researched by the Strategy Working Group of the Lausanne Committee for World Evangelization, which he also led.

We discovered a rather hidden group of people out there—intercessors, who would pray their knees to the bone if given a challenge that fit in with the will of God! They sprang out of the woodwork in nations worldwide. We challenged some to go to the unreached people and to pray on site for them to be evangelized. And they did.

I remember receiving a phone call from the intercessors in Guatemala asking to be sent to the hardest place on our list! So I assigned them to the Maldives. They could pray aloud anyplace in Spanish without being kicked out. And that they did. Remember, they had to book and pay all their own expenses. We were just the clearinghouse for assigning the teams.

When certain nations would not granted visas, there were intercessors from other nations at the ready to go. Today the number is down to about 550 unreached people groups, so an incredible job was done all by volunteers, at their own expense. Dissemination of information was the key, and Peter was able to be that link.

From then on, intercession became an important teaching topic and a vast army of hidden jewels were exposed for their true value in the Body of Christ. All of this was accomplished while Peter was carrying on a full load of teaching in the School of World

Mission. I was COO of Global Harvest Ministries, and my very able assistant, Jean VanEngen, produced all of the newsletters. There were no computers or email in those days, so getting the word out involved mimeograph and fax machines and telephones, plus a bunch of wonderful Fuller Seminary student volunteers who stuffed letters into envelopes by the thousands. They worked long hours on end for a soda, piece of pizza or sandwich, and a cookie. Actually this process had a wonderful, unexpected side benefit, as one of those seminary students met and fell in love with our daughter, Becky, and they have now been married more than twenty-four years!

Peter was actively working on three themes when his time ran out. He longed to see what he termed as "The Great Transfer of Wealth," and wrote some about it in various books. He had a file of close to a dozen innovative projects that promised to produce huge sums of money for the Kingdom of God, and he had been asked to help distribute that wealth to places that could really produce a good spiritual return. Not a cent was ever forthcoming during his lifetime and it was a huge disappointment. He personally invested in a few of them, but at the time it was "money we could afford to lose," and we did.

He longed to see great progress made with Christians moving on up in the Seven Mountain Theory that Lance Wallnau so aptly teaches. That should be catching on faster than it is, and I pray that folks take that teaching seriously and stick with clawing their way up to becoming influencers for Christ in their "mountain" of business, arts and entertainment including Hollywood, our government, and wherever they can help change the current corrupt culture for a godly one.

Peter was also working on "the micro church." So many churches as we have known them in the past are closing, and Christian folks simply don't attend anymore. But there is beginning a little move of God with smaller groups holding church while meeting on different days of the week in odd places like golf clubs, factories, offices, and the like. He wanted to analyze that and offer suggestions to keep them heading in the right direction, I believe. That's all I know about that. He may have discussed this further with some colleagues when I was not present.

So if there was to have been more in this chapter or not, I will never know. Let me just conclude this chapter by saying that Peter was anxious to use his influence and gifts to help others succeed in their callings and be their best for the Kingdom, and that he did very well. It is my firm belief that he now resides with that "great cloud of witnesses" cheering on those of us he left behind to carry on his legacy.

Now back to Peter...

6

PLAN TO FINISH WELL

You probably have not heard many lectures on how to finish your life well. When I turned 82, I decided I qualified to study this and teach on it.

On my 80th birthday, I allowed my family and friends to hold a birthday party. I received hundreds of cards, emails, notes, photos, and even a large album of memories. I was amused by one of the cards I received that said on the front: Here is a crucial question: What do 80-year-old men wear—briefs or boxers? The inside of the card: DEPENDS! Why are senior citizens the only minority demographic group in America who doesn't care if you tell jokes about them?

Let's get back to finishing well, and let's look at five interrelated topics that give us a pretty clear picture of this issue of finishing well.

1. The *challenge* of finishing well.
2. The *pathway* toward finishing well.
3. The *alternative* to finishing well.
4. Eight personal *goals* toward finishing well.
5. The *end* of finishing well—dying well.

The *Challenge* of Finishing Well

No one has verbalized the challenge of finishing well better than the apostle Paul in First Corinthians 9:24-27. The Message translation of the Bible says:

You've all been to the stadium and seen the athletes race. Run to win. All good athletes train hard. They do it for a gold medal that tarnishes and fades. You're after one that's gold eternally. I don't know about you, but I'm running hard for the finish line. I'm giving it everything I've got. No lazy living for me! I'm staying alert and in top condition. I'm not going to get caught napping, telling everyone else all about it and then missing out myself.

I know that you want to run to win! This is not a message for senior citizens only. Paul is referencing the Ancient Olympic Games (776 BC). Many Olympic athletes start training at age 8 to finish at age 30. Eight is 30 percent of the 30 years. If you think you will finish by about 70, then start preparing for finishing at age 21, which is 30 percent.

But it is never too late to start preparing to finish well. I learned one of my most important lessons at age 72: "There is no success without a successor!" I had never heard anyone teaching on finishing well. So let's be practical and realistic. I suggest you start training to finish the race well when you are 35 to 40 years of age.

I like the following quote from Bob Buford's book *Halftime*:

> Recently I have begun looking at my own life through the metaphor of a football game (actually any sport that divides its action into two haves will do). Up until my thirty-fifth year, I was in the first half. Then circumstances intervened that sent me into halftime. Now I am playing the second half and it's turning into a great game.[1]

This is when it starts, but when does it end? For some it ends prematurely. Let me indicate two examples:

Wally Herron was the pioneer of all missionary aviation. He was a member of my mission, the Bolivian Indian Mission (the name later changed to the Andes Evangelical Mission). He was decorated by the Bolivian government with the prestigious "Condor of the Andes" award in recognition of his humanitarian service to the villagers of the Beni region of Bolivia. He airlifted many very ill people out of secluded jungle areas to cities where they could receive the care they needed. He and his wife, Emily, also ran a leper colony where those afflicted with this disease could receive treatment and live a fairly normal life. However, as he was transporting a new plane to further his work, the plane crashed and Wally died at 58 years of age.

Jim Elliott's story is famous. He was a missionary to the Auca Indians, a hostile, unreached tribe of eastern Ecuador. The well-known book *Through Gates of Splendor,* so beautifully written by his widow, Elizabeth, fully documents this tragic story. Jim Elliott and four other young missionaries were speared to death along a riverbank. This occurred just days before Doris and I left for our first missionary assignment in eastern Bolivia in early 1956. Jim was only 28 years old.

Both Wally and Jim received a hero's reward. They both finished well. Now, I am not going to pray that you get a hero's reward. But for most people, it is a long race. My suggestion is to hang in there and plan to run the whole race well. It will be a challenge.

The question then becomes, why is this a challenge? My good friend and colleague mentioned previously, Dr. Bobby Clinton, did some amazing research. He delivered his findings in the Lincoln Seminary Lectures of 1996 entitled, "Focused Lives." The following are the results of the research he undertook:

> The Bible mentions approximately 1,000 leaders. Clinton chose the 100 most prominent ones. Only half (49) had enough information to let us know how they finished. Of these, less than 25% (1 of 4) finished well!

The same holds true for Christian leadership today. It is a challenge! But I like the determination of the apostle Paul cited at the beginning of this chapter when he says, *"I am not going to miss out."* Let's agree with that determination.

The *Pathway* Toward Finishing Well.

The best picture I have found that lays out the pathway toward finishing well is in the book mentioned previously, *The Making of a Leader* by my friend Bobby Clinton. This pathway presents itself in six phases[2]:

Phase I: Sovereign Foundations

Phase II: Inner Life Growth

Phase III: Ministry Maturing

Phase IV: Life Maturing

Phase V: Convergence

Phase VI: Afterglow

For more than 30 years (ages 48-80) I concentrated on convergence. This was the most important guide for my time management and life development over three decades. We defined convergence previously, but to refresh the memory, here is Bobby Clinton's definition taken from *The Making of a Leader*:

> In Convergence, Phase V, God moves the leader into a role that matches his or her gift mix and experience so that ministry

is maximized. The leader uses the best he has to offer and is freed from ministry for which he is not gifted or suited. Many leaders do not experience Convergence.[3]

You will also recall that we noted that the foundation of Convergence has two parts: (1) understanding and applying your spiritual gifts; and (2) understanding and applying your personality and temperament.

Bob Buford, in his book *Halftime,* has a long list of steps along this pathway. The following are five of them[4]:

1. Delegate—at work, play, and home. ... Work smarter, not harder.

2. Do what you do best; drop the rest. ... Go with your strengths. (This would relate to spiritual gifts.)

3. Know when to say no. ...You want to pursue *your* mission, not someone else's. (The most powerful word in Convergence is "NO.")

4. Set limits. Reallocate time to your *mission,* to your core issues. (Some continually say "I don't have time." Yes you do!)

5. Work with people you like. In my second half, I want to work with people who add energy to life, not with those who take energy away.

After thirty years in Convergence, I started Afterglow at age 80. What is Afterglow? Harking back to Bobby Clinton's chart, we see Afterglow is Phase VI. He states it like this:

> For a very few there is Phase VI, Afterglow. The fruit of a lifetime of ministry and growth culminates in an era of recognition and indirect influence at broad levels. Leaders in Afterglow have built up a lifetime of contacts and continue to exert influence in these relationships. Others will seek them out because of their consistent track record in following God. Their storehouse of wisdom gathered over a lifetime of leadership will continue to bless and benefit many.[5]

Here is where Clinton gets the name: "Afterglow is a picture word—it takes us to a fire, which has burned down to a large set of glowing embers. Light and heat are still coming from this fire, which is in its finishing stages ("70+ Focused Life Lived Out" p.

4). Blacksmiths use the hot coals for molding their metals. I have a wood-heated log cabin. The right kind of wood burns all night in the potbelly stove.

Part of the pathway to finishing well is to verbalize your desired legacy. It will give you a compass point for the future. I have stated my desired legacy as follows:

> *I (Peter Wagner) want to be remembered as one who, over the years, accurately heard what the Spirit was saying to the churches, and who faithfully communicated it to leaders of the Body of Christ.*

The *Alternative* to Finishing Well

This is the other side of the coin. Why would I bring up this brief point? Because a huge majority of the U.S. workforce, including Christians, look forward to one thing above all: *retirement!*

They do not see their work as ministry. They see it as a means toward an end: self-indulgence! Of course there are exceptions—some finish one career and begin another aimed at helping others. More about that later. But 10,000 Americans retire every day!

Bob Buford wrote another very interesting book titled *Finishing Well*.[6] In that book, he interviewed 60 successful Christian businesspeople and posed the same question to each person: "What does retirement mean to you?" The answers were both creative and consistent. Here are some samples:

> Wally Hawley, venture capitalist. "Wally, tell me what you think of when I say the word 'retirement.'" Wally responded, "It could mean one of several things, none of which I want to do. The first is to go play golf and just tune out. Another is just sort of dropping out, hanging around, gardening, or watching television. But the common denominator is that in every case, you're not doing anything purposeful or beneficial."[7]

> Millard Fuller, Habitat for Humanity. Knowing very well that the word "retirement" is not in Millard's vocabulary, I asked him, "Millard, have you ever heard about this thing called 'retirement'?"

> "Sure I have," he said with a laugh. "I remember the words of Jesus, who said, "Take up your cross until you are sixty-five,

then lay it down, then take up your fishing pole and move to Florida!"

I said, "You'd think retirement would be in the Bible if God had thought it was important, wouldn't you?"

"Yes, I agree," he responded. "It's pretty clear that when God calls somebody, it's for the duration: You're called to be faithful in that calling for as long as you're able."[8]

Randy Best, founder and president of dozens of businesses. At the end of our conversation, I had one more question for Randy. "When I say the word 'retirement' what comes to your mind?"

He smiled and said, "Well, I know what the term means but—and this is probably unfair—it says to me that you want to live your life completely selfishly. A retired person is just living for himself; that's how I see it. They have put off doing the things they always wanted to do when they were younger and now they are spending their remaining years satisfying their personal whims and desires. I can't even imagine that for myself. What do you do? You travel? You play golf? I can't even imagine not having a purpose beyond just living out my remaining years in such an aimless, self-indulgent sort of way."[9]

Now, let's get a *positive spin.*

Dan Sullivan of Creative Coach Program contrasts "Reactive Retirement vs. Creative Retirement." Dan says, "Reactive retirement is buying into the whole notion that your active time on this planet is really up after about sixty or so. So, you leave the real world, and then you live off your investments. You're no longer building: you're living 'off of,' and you just hope that you die before you run out of assets."

"Well," he said, "that doesn't fly in my book. If you look up the word 'retire' in the dictionary, one of the prominent definitions is 'to take out of use.' When you retire, you're taken out of use, which is a pretty sad statement. Psychologically, that idea has a profound effect on people. What does it mean to be useless? That's reactive retirement."

"Then what do you recommend?" I asked.

"What I call creative retirement. At The Strategic Coach we say, 'We want you to decide to retire today. Begin a new life after today. We want you to retire from everything you dislike doing and focus your attention totally on what you love doing.'

"What I want to do," Dan said, "is to challenge everyone who has an ounce of energy left to get rid of all notions of reactive retirement. The answer to finishing well is creative retirement, which, if you do it right, isn't retirement at all but plunging into some of the most important work you'll ever do."[10]

So I personally decided to do this when I turned 80. I don't want to retire, I want to re+fire!

The very week I finished preparing this lesson, the entire *Forbes* magazine of March 4, 2013, was on retirement. Let me quote a paragraph from one of the articles:

> Conventional retirement is rapidly going the way of the Oldsmobile and Saturday mail delivery. Hardly anyone working today envisions themselves checking out

their final years living on a fixed pension in a sunshine state. Indeed, the coming generation isn't really planning on retiring at all—they expect to keep traveling, saving and giving back well into their eighth and ninth decades. Call it antiretirement.[11]

Just as an aside, I also found this interesting paragraph in *Forbes* magazine:

Researchers at INSERM, the French government's health research agency, studied 429,000 retirees in France who were formerly self-employed and discovered that their risk of having a diagnosis of dementia was reduced by 3.2% for each extra year they worked before retirement.[12]

Eight Personal *Goals* Toward Finishing Well

1. *Cultivate a Mature Christian Character*

Here is what the apostle Paul said when he knew he was finishing, *"the Holy Spirit testifies in every city, saying that chains and tribulations await me. But none of these things move me; nor do I count my life dear to myself,* **so that I may finish my race with joy**...*"* (Acts 20:23-24).

By the time you finish you will have had time to develop two character qualities above all—humility and holiness.

In the same chapter from Acts, Luke records Paul as saying, *"And when they had come to him, he said to them: 'You know, from the first day that I came to Asia, in what manner I always lived among you, serving the Lord with all **humility**...'"* (Acts 20:18-19). Holiness was Paul's first requirement for Christian leadership, as he wrote to Timothy, *"A bishop then must be **blameless**"* (1 Timothy 3:2). Paul also said this to the Corinthians: *"For I know **nothing against myself**..."* (1 Corinthians 4:4). The New Living Translation says, *"My conscience is clear...."*

2. Manage Your Succession

I was 72 years of age when I heard it said that, "There is no success without a successor." At the time, I was leading twelve organizations and had no plans for successors. I began to move on this and by the year 2010 (when I was 80), I had:

- Dissolved two of the organizations.
- Chosen successors and turned over nine of the organizations to spiritual sons and daughters.

- Kept one, which was my Eagle's Vision Apostolic Team, which was my personal team and no successor was possible. I assumed it would disband at my death.

My good friend John Maxwell has analyzed this so very well in his book, *The 21 Irrefutable Laws of Leadership*. The last law he analyzes, Law # 21, is The Law of Legacy. He writes:

> Of all the laws of leadership, the Law of Legacy is the one that the fewest leaders seem to learn. What is it? Every leader eventually leaves his organization—one way or another. He may change jobs, get promoted, or retire. And even if a person refuses to retire, he is going to die. My lasting value, like that of any leader, would be measured by my ability to give the organization a smooth succession.[13]

Maxwell goes on to say, "When it is a leader's time to leave the organization, he has got to be willing to walk away and let his successor do his own thing. Meddling only hurts him and the organization."[14]

I don't like to dwell much on failure, but one of America's most famous pastors trained his son for twenty-five years to be his successor, and finally installed him as senior pastor. But when his son started making changes to minister to the new generation, his father didn't like it and forced him to resign. The whole enterprise went bankrupt and eventually fell apart and disbanded.

My successors have changed every one of the nine organizations; and I must say, all are for the better. They are doing things I never wanted to or would have been able to do. I am ecstatic! And, so are they!

3. Learn to be Number 2

In all of my organizations, I was Number 1! Now, I have joined Global Spheres Inc. Chuck Pierce is Number 1 and I am Number 2. I am still working on this one.

--- • • • ---

Doris here, interjecting some historical information that may or may not be of interest to you, the reader. Peter and I lived very happily in our dream home in a pine forest in Colorado Springs at the foot of Pike's Peak and the beautiful Rocky Mountains for twenty years. We had built that dream home and were basking in the beauty that surrounded us. We had eight acres of ponderosa pines and Peter loved the woods behind our home. He built trails for our

4-wheeers all through the woods, and we named each road after a person in our extended family.

He loved working out in the woods every Saturday morning, clearing and upgrading things around the authentic 1800s log cabin we bought from a neighbor and reinstalled in the center of the woods along the ruts of an ancient stagecoach path up to Denver that passed through our land. Peter named it The Stagecoach Stop. Kids loved to stay there. We even installed a functional outhouse off to the side of the cabin that we moved down from my daughter's ranch in Wyoming. How we loved our Colorado home!

Peter continued to travel and teach, both nationally and internationally, especially at the Wagner Leadership Institute, one of the mentioned organizations that he founded and led. After a trip to teach at WLI in Korea in January 2013, he became violently ill with a lung infection that progressed to the point that it was difficult for him to breathe at our 7,300 foot-high home perched in the Rocky Mountains. It was also the beginning of the heart failure that eventually took his life.

Chuck Pierce, at that point, offered to move us to Texas to a much lower altitude to help prolong

Peter's life and comfort. Chuck graciously got us moved and kept Peter on the Glory of Zion/Global Spheres payroll until he died, two years after our move to Texas. Chuck provided us with the best possible medical insurance and we lacked nothing. I continue on as one of the ministers, working in the field of deliverance, and plan to do so as long as I am able. We are so very grateful for Chuck's generosity, concern and care. He has kept me on Glory of Zion payroll and I continue to do deliverances a few times a week. I teach deliverance for Wagner University and do seminars on the topic when invited by other ministries. I purchased an RV equipped for a handicapped person and traveled from coast to coast doing seminars and personal deliverances. In 2020 I had to cancel twelve seminars when the COVID-19 pandemic hit, due to quarantine. But I keep busy, and plan to work as long as I am able. God has graciously kept my mind sharp, so I plan to "die with my boot (I only have one leg) on."

Back to Peter's notes:

4. *Get Your Finances in Order*

Honor the next generation.

Officially retain three professionals:

- *A financial planner* will help you build a retirement fund. Although our fund is modest, it has been very helpful for several large emergency items that have arisen since widowhood, and has been a huge blessing.

- *A family attorney.* Get your wills written and in order with powers of attorney and medical directives, and estate planning documents. Excellent professional advice is needed here.

- *A tax accountant* will keep everything in order, and all payments current.

———————

I, Doris, have asked a good personal friend, a Christian professional financial planner to write a final chapter to conclude this book on how to go about doing this. I must confess that Peter and I could have done a better job of my involvement in our financial matters. For most of our married life we worked together all day and when we came home in the evenings, he would head to his desk to care for the family finances, bill paying, and all of the related paperwork. I would head to the kitchen to prepare dinner. There was a distinct division of labor.

He tried to coach me during his last few weeks of life, but it was a lot for me to absorb. I now wish that transition had taken a little longer and I were more involved. I could have used more practical information and help, so I have asked Peter Roselle to provide that for you. Peter has spent many years in finance, is a dear personal friend, a pastor of a vibrant church in New Jersey, a great musician, and just a wonderful Christian brother. I would like to help people be as prepared as possible for the two sure things—death and taxes!

I remember vividly that our then family attorney in Colorado Springs suggested that as a kindness to our daughters, we prepay our funerals and purchase a grave plot so as to keep them from that difficult chore when the time came. We did just that, and even picked out a headstone. Peter designed it and wanted something very modest. We chose a grave plot as close as possible to the grave of the stillborn daughter of Jack and Becky Sytsema, our youngest daughter. It was about 200 paces down a knoll from the children's grave area in Evergreen Cemetery in Colorado Springs, where little Anna was laid to rest.

After our headstone was in place, Peter and I took our girls out to see it one day when they were all together. Rather than the morose atmosphere we expected, they all jumped out of the car with their cameras, snapped a bunch of photos and rejoiced openly, much to our surprise. They were so grateful that we had done that. We had picked out our matching caskets and the whole nine yards.

Actually, when we moved to Texas, we put up our Colorado grave plots for sale and they were sold quite quickly. When Peter passed away, the policy we bought transferred to a funeral home in Texas with no problems. I found another suitable plot, which I am very happy with. I actually received a $400 refund when the dust settled because I did not use a limo service for the burial. My grandson, Chris Potter, who lives in Colorado, was able to collect our gravestone and transport it here in his pickup truck. It was properly placed shortly after Peter's burial. The lovely, well-cared-for cemetery is only about a fifteen minute drive from our home. We decorate the grave differently every few months, and give away our nice, used flowers to empty vases on headstones near Peter's grave.

Now back to Peter's notes…

5. Keep Learning

Don't get stuck in the mud—look for new horizons. In one of my own latest books, *This Changes Everything,* I explain in great detail 17 paradigm shifts I have made in my Christian walk. I have always been a curious, investigative individual, so I may undergo a few more before I am called Home to Glory! Keeping an active mind by reading, studying, and continually learning keeps one growing in mind, spirit, and intellect.

6. Make Time for People

John Castle, a Dallas attorney said concerning finishing well, "I want to see myself…with more time for people—upbeat, positive, and cheerful. And I plan to get more intentional about that."

In Bobby Clinton's thoughts on Afterglow, he states, "Others will seek them out because of their consistent track record in following God." Doris and I have been discovering this. Our problem is that we are not "people persons," so are not very hospitable. But I am keeping a list of younger people who are seeking me out just to pick my brain and spend a bit of time with me, and I am making room for that in these last years of my life.

7. Write Your Memoirs

Writing your memoir is not pride, it is inter-generational impartation.

Warning: Do not wait until the end! It took me three years to write mine and was finally published on my 80th birthday. It is titled *Wrestling with Alligators, Prophets, and Theologians.* (At this writing, it is out of print but still available used on Amazon .com).

Doris is almost finished writing her memoirs, planned to be published by Destiny Image in 2022. It is taking her much longer. She began in 2011, but got stuck when she started to chronicle the prayer movement we led during the decade of the 1990s. So much was accomplished during that decade that she felt it was difficult to write about it without it sounding like bragging. It started out as sort of a history of her parents and grandparents just for our three girls to have and pass along to their children. I have no doubt it will be cherished by family but also of great interest to many far and wide.

8. Plan More Time for Leisure

I am a promoter of "apostolic leisure." Leisure is not automatic and your most important word is "NO!" Doris and I had to learn this. We will spend our latter years together and plan to enjoy a:

- Week on Maui with our girls using accrued airline miles
- Week with our California daughter near Christmas
- Week at "Tulip Time" with our Michigan daughter in May, bringing our three daughters together
- Week on our annual "Wagner Wine Tour" with close friends and family. Our last one was in Argentina visiting Malbec vineyards. Our very dear friends Brian and Lori Kooiman coordinate these tours.

Now, having completed those eight personal goals for Finishing Well, let's return to the main outline and major goal Number 5: The *End* of Finishing Well—Dying Well.

There is not much preaching on dying well. Why? Some push "negative confession" to the extreme of denying death. But both old age and death are realities—not the result of "negative confession." Don't indulge in pathological denial.

Billy Graham addressed this issue in his book *Nearing Home*. He was 93 and he describes old age. I (at the time Peter wrote this) am 82, but I am old (Peter died at age 86 after a lengthy battle with heart disease). I love Afterglow, but I don't like old age. As I am living much longer than my father did, one of my great surprises in the aging process has been the loss of strength to do the simplest things: getting up from a chair; having endurance to visit with someone longer than an hour; or just going to the doctor's office.

But no matter who you are, nothing will halt the onset of old age completely and, like it or not, the longer you live the more its burdens and disabilities will become your companions. Rather than deny the realities and ravages of old age, it is far better to admit them and prepare for them—and by God's grace, even welcome them as part of His plan for life.

Doris and I have decided to admit the "ravages of old age" and prepare for them.

Some practical things to remember, in fact a guiding principle: Don't be a burden to your kids.

Grieving is enough! Don't leave them with a lot of headaches!

Here are some things we have done:

1. We have prepaid our funerals, even chosen our matching caskets.
2. We have long-term care insurance.
3. Our girls know about our finances.

   - They know our financial planner and family attorney.
   - They know our wills—no surprises.
   - They have medical power of attorney.
   - They know the executor of our estate.

In Scripture, the apostle Paul was never in denial. He knew he was going to die. He made the following positive confession:

> *You take over. I'm about to die, my life an offering on God's altar. This is the only race worth running. I've run hard right to the finish, believed all the way. All that's left now is the shouting—God's applause! Depend on it, he's an honest judge. He'll do right not*

only by me, but by everyone eager for his coming (2 Timothy 4:6-8 The Message).

———◆◆◆———

And let me (Doris) add this concerning Peter as I write this several years after his death. He is now rejoicing with that "great cloud of witnesses" cheering on those loved ones he left behind, but as the one closest to him in his lifetime, he absolutely reflected what Paul said to Timothy, *"I have fought the good fight, I have finished the race, I have kept the faith"* (2 Timothy 4:7).

Notes

1. Bob Buford, *Halftime: Changing Your Game Plan from Success to Significance* (Grand Rapids, MI: Zondervan, 1995), 19.
2. J. Robert Clinton, T*he Making of a Leader, 2ⁿᵈ Edition* (Colorado Springs, CO: NavPress, 2012), 17.
3. Ibid., 38.
4. Buford, *Halftime,* 132-133.
5. Clinton, *The Making of a Leader*, 40.
6. Bob Buford, *Finishing Well* (Brentwood, TN: Integrity Publishers, 2004).
7. Ibid., 30.
8. Ibid., 173-174.
9. Ibid., 140.

10. Ibid.

11. Janet Novack, "Retire Rich: The Forbes 2013 Antiretirement Guide," Forbes magazine, March 4, 2013, https://www.forbes.com/sites/janetnovack/2013/02/13/retire-rich-the-forbes-2013-antiretirement-guide/?sh=14c5ffd9226a; accessed March 10, 2021.

12. Richard Eisenberg, "Retiring Later Could Help You Fend Off Alzheimer's," Forbes magazine, July 15, 2012; https://www.forbes.com/sites/nextavenue/2013/07/15/retiring-later-could-help-you-fend-off-alzheimers/?sh=6ecc86281766; accessed March 10, 2021.

13. John Maxwell, *The 21 Irrefutable Laws of Leadership* (Nashville, TN: Thomas Nelson, 1998), 220-222.

14. Ibid.

7

SPECIAL BONUS CHAPTER

A STRONG FINANCIAL FINISH

Mission-Minded and Vision-Driven

by Peter Roselle

*I press toward the mark for the prize of
the high calling of God in Christ Jesus.*
—PHILIPPIANS 3:14

*"I don't plan on relaxing on the front
porch in a rocking chair. I much prefer an
airplane seat. I'm currently working on four
million frequent flyer miles, and five million
sounds like a pretty good target to me."*
—C. PETER WAGNER, age 80

I am grateful to Doris for asking me to contribute this chapter on the topic of achieving a strong financial finish. Both Peter and Doris have had an enormous and positive impact on my life. I met them in 2004 when Peter took an interest in my role as a "tentmaker." I have been working in the financial services industry in the New York City area since 1983. Since 1999, I have also been overseeing King of Kings, the Apostolic Center that my wife, Trisha, and I founded in Basking Ridge, New Jersey.

In 2007, Peter and Chuck Pierce commissioned me as a marketplace apostle and commissioned Trisha as a prophet. We both received impartations that day that shifted us into higher dimensions of Kingdom revelation and insight. As Peter's colleague, apprentice, and advisor, I was blessed to see his transformation from someone who carried traces of a "poverty mindset," developed after sixteen years of missionary work, into the deeper revelation of prosperity for the purpose of advancing God's Kingdom on earth.

This chapter is being written during the COVID-19 crisis in 2020. Large, well-known companies are filing for bankruptcy, the U.S. has taken on a staggering amount of additional debt. We know that "this too shall pass," but we don't know when, or the staggering final tally of losses that will be incurred.

In many cases, the plans people made to retire must be put on hold because of the increased risk and uncertainty in global stock markets. We take heart in the saying, "We may not know what the future holds, but we know God holds our future." The pandemic has placed the need for financial planning front and center. Proverbs 16:9 says, *"A man's heart plans his way, but the Lord directs his steps."* We are told to make plans; but just as the Israelites followed the cloud by day and fire by night to escape the bondage of Egypt, we must consistently be in search of Holy Spirit's *kairos* guidance to avoid catastrophe and be delivered from evil (Matthew 6:13).

There is a frequently quoted statistic that says the Bible has more than 2,000 verses related to the topic of finances. The following are a few that I feel closely correlate with a strong financial finish:

- We must *"seek first the kingdom of God,"* and trust that He will provide all our needs. (Matthew 6:33).

- We must remind ourselves, *"Unless the Lord builds the house"* we will be laboring in vain (Psalm 127:1).

- We are *in the world but not of the world* (John 17:16), so we must be wise and avoid being *"unequally yoked with unbelievers"* in business partnerships (2 Corinthians 6:14).

- We must hold our possessions loosely, for *"to whom much is given much will be required"* (Luke 12:48).

- How we handle our finances is a direct reflection of our highest priorities; *"Where your treasure is, there your heart will be also"* (Matthew 6:21).

- The biblical concept of stewardship posits that everything we have belongs to the Lord and that we will be asked to give an account of our stewardship (Luke 16:2).

- What do you have that God hasn't given you? And if everything you have is from God, why boast as though it were not a gift? (1 Corinthians 4:7)

- When we prove ourselves faithful with little we will be trusted with more (Luke 16:10).

- We are warned often that trusting in our wealth instead of trusting God is a primary idolatrous deception.

No one can serve two masters; for either he will hate the one and love the other, or else he will be loyal to the one and despise the other. You cannot serve God and mammon (Matthew 6:24).

*Teach those who are rich in this world not to be proud **and not to trust in their money,** which is so unreliable. Their trust should be in God, who richly gives us all we need for our enjoyment* (1 Timothy 6:17 NLT).

For the love of money is a root of all kinds of evil (1 Timothy 6:10).

- God gives us the ability to get wealth for the purpose of expanding His Kingdom on earth.

You shall remember the Lord your God, for it is He who gives you power to get wealth, that He may establish His covenant which

He swore to your fathers, as it is this day (Deuteronomy 8:18).

- God blesses our obedience when our financial priorities are properly aligned:

Bring all the tithes into the storehouse, that there may be food in My house, and try Me now in this," says the Lord of hosts, "If I will not open for you the windows of heaven and pour out for you such blessing that there will not be room enough to receive it (Malachi 3:10).

For the eyes of the Lord run to and fro throughout the whole earth, to show Himself strong on behalf of those whose heart is loyal to Him… (2 Chronicles 16:9).

- Joseph was such a good steward that Potiphar trusted him with all his possessions (Genesis 39).
- Our contentment comes through a committed relationship to God, not the amount of our possessions:

For what shall it profit a man, if he gains the whole world, and loses his own soul? (Mark 8:36)

...I have learned in whatever state I am, to be content: I know how to be abased, and I know how to abound. Everywhere and in all things I have learned both to be full and to be hungry, both to abound and to suffer need. I can do all things through Christ who strengthens me (Philippians 4:11-13).

After thirty-five years in finance, I am always happy to give practical advice about biblical stewardship, financial planning, budgeting, and investing, and will include resources to help in those areas. But I felt the Lord prompting me to devote the rest of this chapter to using Peter and Doris' example to motivate you to develop a new mental wineskin for why it is important to have a strong financial finish.

Peter and Doris are both role models for the subtitle of this chapter, "Mission-Minded and Vision-Driven." Not only were they literally missionaries for sixteen years in Bolivia, they have lived their lives with the mission to advance God's Kingdom and *"destroy the works of the devil"* (1 John 3:8).

What about you?

Do you feel like you have a clear understanding of your mission and a clear vision of how to accomplish it? If not, I encourage you to press in and contend for a download of God's blueprints for your life. Instead of just working to earn a paycheck, imagine yourself in a position that optimizes your strengths and brings more meaning and purpose to your work. When you find the place where your skills overlap with your passion in a sphere that can generate sufficient income, you have reached what Peter referred to as "convergence."

He wrote in his booklet titled *The Fourth Career*, "In a nutshell, convergence means that you finally get to the place where almost everything you do, at least professionally, is rooted in the gifts and the personality or temperament that God has given you." In convergence, your work is more fulfilling, less exhausting, and allows you to go beyond the typical U.S. retirement age of 65. Peter and Doris never retired! Convergence helped them increase their effectiveness in their later years.

The following is another quote from *The Fourth Career* that Peter wrote at age 80, on his thoughts about retirement:

My hope and plan is that in the Fourth Career I will be able to continue to remain active in fulfilling the assignments that God has given me for advancing His kingdom positively, and never need to be "put out to pasture." I have begun contemplating the meaning of the word "emeritus." For instance, Ché Ahn is now the Chancellor of Wagner Leadership Institute, and I have become Chancellor Emeritus. What does this mean for me? Admittedly, I haven't checked it out carefully, but I have concluded that the word "emeritus" must mean "rocking chair" in Latin. I don't like that thought very much. I don't plan on relaxing on the front porch in a rocking chair. I much prefer an airplane seat. I'm currently working on four million frequent flyer miles, and five million sounds like a pretty good target to me.

As Christians we understand from Scripture that God loves us with a father's love and wants what is best for His children. Jeremiah 29:11 says, *"'I know the plans I have for you,' declares the Lord, 'plans to prosper you and not to harm you, plans to give you hope and a future.'"* Jeremiah 1:4-5 (New International Version) says, *"The word of the Lord came to me, saying, 'Before I formed you in the womb I knew you, before you were born I set you apart; I appointed you as a prophet to the nations.'"*

Mark Twain is credited with saying, "The most important day of your life is not the day you were born; it is the day you find out WHY you were born." I hope this bears witness with you, because the next question is, "Why were YOU born?" Paul described his mission this way in Philippians 3:12, *"Not that I have already attained, or am already perfected; but I press on, that I may lay hold of that for which Christ Jesus has also laid hold of me."*

Do you believe God laid hold of you for a purpose? Do you know what that purpose is? We are no different from Paul or Jeremiah; God's plan for our lives was established while we were still in our mother's womb. Make it your goal to discover your unique mission and receive God's ever-unfolding vision that will allow you to complete it. As this happens you will stress less over finances because, like every good father, He will help fund your efforts to complete His plan for your life.

Peter never stopped exploring new ideas and drilling down into the core of concepts that tested his conventional thinking. I call this trait a "fascination with wonder." He was willing to continually reintegrate his thinking with the unfolding revelations he was receiving from the Lord. He came to understand that God's mission for him was much bigger than he had originally imagined. Peter's domain of expertise at Fuller Theological Seminary was missiology, defined as, "the theological study of the mission of the church, especially the character and purpose of missionary work." He soon realized that, in addition to focusing on traditional evangelism and local church growth, there was a larger calling to disciple nations and expand the influence of God's Kingdom on earth.

Whenever Peter saw evidence that his conventional wisdom did not align with his new understanding of the Kingdom, he immersed himself in research to find out where he needed to adjust his thinking. He was challenged to test these Kingdom concepts by a fellow professor at Fuller named George Eldon Ladd, who wrote extensively about the Kingdom of God.[1] He also had friends, including Ed Silvoso, who were modeling a much larger and more culturally engaging approach to "ministry" than the traditional path of graduating from Bible school and working on staff in a local church.

I mention all this because achieving a strong financial finish is much more likely if you cultivate a similar Kingdom mindset and stoke your own fascination with wonder. Why? When you think of Peter and Doris, does the word *retire* come to mind? At this writing Doris is 88 years old and is still traveling around the country in an RV to hold deliverance workshops. Peter was teaching and writing until the end of his life. In John 20:21 Jesus says, *"Peace to you! As the Father has sent Me, I also send you."* Peter and Doris answered that call and along the way expanded their mission from a local-church mindset to a Kingdom mindset.

In my case, the conventional wisdom would have defined what I do as "bi-vocational." The traditional track would be for my wife and I to plant and grow the church so I could leave my secular job and go into "full-time ministry." That is a valid and biblically sound career path; yet the apostle Paul modified it by continuing to work in his trade as a tentmaker (Acts 18:3). Even though he could have asked for financial support, he said, *"So then, where is my reward? It is found in continually depositing the good news into people's hearts, without obligation, free of charge, and not insisting on my rights to be financially supported"* (1 Corinthians 9:18 TPT).

Peter felt the term "marketplace apostle," was a much better description for Paul than "bi-vocational." Paul brought the gospel into his work sphere—they were not two separate domains. Paul did not have the goal to "quit his secular job to go into the full-time ministry." His secular job was an important part of his ministry because it kept him close to the lost and hurting people in his region and kept his message relevant to them.

In Acts 19:12 we are told that when Paul was in Ephesus, *"even handkerchiefs or aprons were brought from his body to the sick, and the diseases left them and the evil spirits went out of them."* As a tentmaker, the "apron" would have been part of Paul's trade, a garment he wore with large pockets to hold his tools and material. The handkerchief would have been what we call a bandana.

After three months trying to preach at the synagogue, we're told in Acts 19:9, *"when some* [Jews] *were hardened and did not believe, but spoke evil of the Way before the multitude, Paul departed from them and withdrew the disciples, reasoning daily in the school of Tyrannus."* Paul would work in the morning and teach during his lunch break when the hall was not being used. The Ephesian believers asked if they could take Paul's bandana and work apron to the people who were too sick to attend the meeting. Acts 19:11 says, *"God worked unusual miracles by the hands of Paul."* This was all done in the marketplace, not inside a church building.

In his book *This Changes Everything,* Peter chronicled seventeen paradigm shifts he experienced over the course of his life. Chapter 17 is titled, "From a Spirit of Poverty to a Spirit of Prosperity." It was an important factor for his own strong financial finish. In the Introduction he wrote: "A paradigm shift inevitably pulls us out of our comfort zones. Just about everybody prefers comfort to discomfort. Maintaining the status quo seems like the best choice."

Peter became a "serial paradigm shifter." He was not embarrassed to modify his opinions on important topics as the Lord unfolded fresh revelation. Once he realized money could be a force for good in God's Kingdom, his idea of *equipping the saints* (Ephesians 4:12), expanded from seminary training to activating church members as marketplace ministers.

The last time I spoke with Peter was in his hospital room three weeks before his death. I was in Texas attending a conference at Glory of Zion. My friend, John Price, and I went to visit Peter knowing it was likely the last time we would see him. As we were leaving his room, he called out to us and said, "When you come back tomorrow, I want you to give me a summary of tonight's sermon, okay?" He never lost his hunger to hear the fresh word of the Lord. Surely, Peter and Doris provide a lesson here for all of us. Like Caleb, they refuse(d) to allow their age and physical constraints to dictate their agenda: Mission-Minded and Vision-Driven.

Are You Ready?

In his later years, before starting a talk, Peter would say, "Are you ready?" We knew that meant he was going to pull an index card from his jacket pocket and read a joke. We would always laugh, both at the joke and at how hard Peter laughed at his own joke. This stern German, Princeton Seminary graduate, PhD professor at Fuller, renowned author of countless books and research papers, never lost his childlike love for the truth. I pray that I will never forget the mischievous sparkle that would appear in Peter's eyes just as he said, "Are you ready?" I can hear him telling us now, "Choose the airplane seat over the rocking chair!" God, help us remain fascinated with wonder until that wonder-filled moment when we meet You face to face.

Practical Steps

The following are practical steps to consider as you journey through your own conversations regarding the wealth God has, and will, entrust to you.

Prioritize Your Expenses

Budgeting and financial planning are two tools you can use to open conversations with your spouse, family, and the Lord regarding the stewardship of your wealth. While the conversations can be awkward or difficult at first, they become doorways for freedom and revelation in the way you view and manage your finances. If you are married, it is important to set aside time to sit down and plan together.

As a starting point, first identify how much income you generate each month. If your income varies from month to month, consider basing your budget on your lowest monthly earnings in the last few months. Don't forget to account for taxes!

Once you have identified how much money you have coming in each month, list your most important expenses. These may include your charitable donations, tithes, and basic living expenses—food, rent, and utilities. When you have identified your basic expenses, set a goal to save or invest a certain amount each month. Having identified these major categories—important expenses, giving, saving, and investing—then move to prioritize other lifestyle expenses such as date nights, eating out, travel, etc.

Mobile Financial Planning Apps

Technology can help you by integrating expense tracking into your daily routine. There are multiple products on the market, so I recommend searching for "Best mobile personal financial planning apps," scroll down past the advertisements and read some reviews about the pros and cons of the different apps listed. They are all effective, but you may have preferences for different features.

Set Up an Investment Strategy

When you determine the minimum amount you want to save or invest each month, it's time to execute. When it comes to investing, keep it simple and easy by setting up automatic monthly contributions. Automatic bank drafts allow you to save diligently and mindlessly. Not many people have enough time to sit down each month and determine what they will contribute to their investment account. Even when they do have the time, they often forget! Set a goal, even if it is small, and invest for the future.

Take the 401(k) Match

A company 401(k) match is free money, so take advantage of it. This is your company incentivizing you to save for *your* retirement. Before you ever think about opening any other kind of retirement account, make sure you take advantage of your company 401(k) match if one is offered.

Open a Roth IRA

After you take the match, then what? Or what if your company does not have a match or does not offer a 401(k) plan? The next step in either scenario is to open a Roth IRA, which is a special retirement account where you pay taxes on money going *into* the account but future *withdrawals are tax-free.* The reason for this is simple—tax-free growth. Uncle

Sam cannot touch this! When you have maxed out your Roth IRA for the year, continue contributing to your 401(k) until you reach the contribution limit for the year. Note: There are income limits associated with your ability to contribute to a Roth IRA, so be sure to talk to a tax or financial professional before proceeding.

Consider a Traditional IRA

If you are making too much to contribute to a Roth IRA, do not have access to a 401(k), or have already maxed out your 401(k), you might consider the Traditional IRA. You can contribute to a Traditional IRA no matter your income level. As an added bonus, you can deduct your contributions to a Traditional IRA from your taxable income. Keep in mind you cannot max out both a Roth IRA and a Traditional IRA. Consider talking to a tax or financial professional if you are unsure which investment vehicle is right for you.

Tax Advice

After thirty-five years in the business, I can say that the vast majority of people are well-served to pay an accountant to prepare their taxes each year. The rules are very complex and continue to change.

You should take your time, interview different candidates, and choose someone you feel understands your situation and cares enough to give you advice in plain English.

Insurance Products and Advice

This is a very important topic to understand since we all must own at least car insurance to legally drive in the U.S. But you need many other types of insurance in the course of your life: property and casualty, medical, life insurance (especially if you are married with children), long-term care, disability, etc. Let's be honest, it is not the most exciting topic in the world, but it can contribute mightily to a strong financial finish. It is important to find an insurance professional who can objectively advise you on the pros and cons of the many different choices available in the market. A gifted insurance advisor will take the time to understand your situation and shop the market to find the best fit for your specific needs. It is worth investing the time to understand the risks that insurance covers.

Create Accountability

It's always great to have a plan, but if there is no execution of the plan, then what's the point? There must be accountability in place when it comes to financial planning. Money is a sensitive subject for many. This is where it may help to have a trusted financial professional—someone to help you walk through the simple and complex financial decisions and always has your best interest in mind. The adviser's number-one priority is to ensure your financial success; and what you share with them is confidential.

Estate Planning—Wills and Trusts

Forgive me for bringing up, as I know some people are not generally fond of this topic. I believe every adult should have a will and medical power of attorney that provides instructions about your medical care in the event of a medical emergency. You may not feel like you have enough assets to justify spending money on a will, but without one you will leave your loved ones with the burden of dealing with your affairs without a road map. If you are married with children, both spouses need to have wills in place.

Like insurance, it is not an exciting or even comfortable topic to discuss, but it is an essential part of loving and caring for your family. Parents with young children also need to name guardians for their children in the will. It is a deeply prayerful decision to approach someone, usually a family member, to ask if they would be willing to serve as guardians (take legal custody) for your children in the event of your death. It will certainly help them handle the financial side of that decision if they know that you have life insurance in place that will help them carry the additional costs.

Reevaluate

Money is a great tool and it can provide a lot of freedom, but it can also become a snare. Whether it is every quarter, every six months, or once a year, take time to intentionally revisit the intentions and motivations of your heart regarding your wealth and to reevaluate your plan.

Trusted Resources for Kingdom Financial Advice

I recommend the following resources when considering how to accomplish a *strong financial finish:*

Kingdom Advisors

National network of Christian financial advisors. https://kingdomadvisors.com/find-a-professional/ directory-search

Books

Wealth to Last: Money Essentials for the Second Half of Life by Larry Burkett and Ron Blue

Master Your Money: A Step-by-Step Plan for Financial Freedom by Ron Blue

National Christian Foundation (NCF)

NCF is the eighth largest charity in the United States, with a mission to leverage generosity through the use of donor-advised-funds and other philanthropic tools. https://ncfgiving.com

Generous Giving

A division of the McClellan Foundation, helping introduce generosity as a lifestyle. I recommend visiting their website to listen to the posted testimonies from Christians around the country. https://generousgiving.org/

Theology of Work

An incredible resource with work-related commentary on every book of the Bible. https://www.theologyofwork.org/

Note

1. Books by George Eldon Ladd include: *The Gospel of the Kingdom; The Presence of the Future; Critical Questions About the Kingdom of God;* and *A Theology of the New Testament.*

ABOUT
PETER ROSELLE

Peter has worked in the financial services industry since 1983. He is a financial advisor for Archetype Wealth Partners where he serves on the Investment Committee and is the portfolio manager for Archetype's ESG portfolios. Peter earned a Bachelor's degree in Economics and a Master's in Business Administration in Finance, both from Seton Hall University. He works with business owners, nonprofit organizations, and corporate executives seeking advice on asset allocation, retirement planning, and estate planning.

Peter is a published author on the topic of sustainable investing, a growing discipline that aims to help investors align their portfolios with their values. He helped launch the New York City affiliate for the National Christian Foundation (NCF), the eighth largest charity in the U.S. NCF's mission is to expand generosity in the Body of Christ using sophisticated proprietary philanthropic tools developed by NCF Founder Terry Parker.

Peter and his wife, Trisha, have been married since 1985. They are both ordained ministers and continue to lead the Apostolic Equipping Center they founded in 1999 at King of Kings Worship Center in Basking Ridge, New Jersey.

ABOUT
C. PETER WAGNER

C. Peter Wagner was the Ambassadorial Apostle of Global Spheres, Inc. (GSI), an apostolic network providing activation and alignment for Kingdom-minded leaders of the Body of Christ. He traveled extensively throughout the world, helping to equip believers to minister in the areas of apostolic ministries, wealth, dominion, and reformation of society. Peter considered this his "fourth career," which he began at the age of 80.

His first career was serving as a missionary to Bolivia, along with his wife, Doris; his second was teaching in the Fuller Seminary School of World Mission (now School of Intercultural Studies); and his third was founding and developing Global Harvest Ministries, which included the world prayer movement and the Wagner Leadership Institute (WLI). WLI has now become Wagner University and has students in the U.S. and twelve other nations.

On October 21, 2016, Peter went home to be with the Lord.